ANOTHER DAY
Paul McCartney
Life Beyond the Beatles

Written by

Pete Chrisp

sona BOOKS

© Danann Media Publishing Limited 2023

First Published Danann Media Publishing Limited 2023
WARNING: For private domestic use only, any unauthorised copying, hiring,
lending or public performance of this book is illegal.

CAT NO: SON0548

Photography courtesy of

Getty images:

Leon Neal/AFP
Universal Images Group
Mark Sennet
Harry Durrant
Samir Hussein/WireImage
Marc Serota
The Asahi Shimbun
Gijsbert Hanekroot/Redferns
Mike Lawn/Evening Standard/Hulton Archive
Evening Standard/Hulton Archive
Daily Express/Hulton Archive
Ian Showell/Keystone/Hulton Archive
ARTCO-Berlin/ullstein bild

Michael Putland
Jones/Daily Express
Mirrorpix
Thierry Orban/Sygma
Rob Verhorst/Redferns
Bettmann
Ian Dickson/Redferns
Robert R. McElroy
Jean-Claude Deutsch/Paris Match
Reg Lancaster/Daily Express/Hulton Archive
Jack Kay/Daily Express/Hulton Archive
Fred Hayes
Michael Ward

Alamy:

Records
Adam Bigg
PA Images
Pictorial Press Ltd

Popimages
Trinity Mirror / Mirrorpix
TheCoverVersion
Goddard Archive

Other images, Wiki Commons

Book design Darren Grice at Ctrl-d

All rights reserved. No Part of this title may be reproduced or transmitted in any material form (including photocopying or storing it in any medium by electronic means and whether or not transiently or incidentally to some other use of this publication) without the written permission of the copyright owner, except in accordance with the provisions of the Copyright, Designs and Patents Act 1988. Applications for the copyright owner's written permission should be addressed to the publisher.

This is an independent publication and it is unofficial and unauthorised and as such has no connection with the artist or artists featured, their management or any other organisation connected in any way whatsoever with the artist or artists featured in the book.

Made in EU.
ISBN: 978-1-915343-08-6

Contents

Introduction: 8

Prologue: 10
1967-69: *The Beginning Of The End*

Chapter 1: 18
1969-70: *The End*

Chapter 2: 26
1970-71: *The New Beginning*

Chapter 3: 38
1971-72: *Ram On*

Chapter 4: 44
1973-74: *Bond On The Run*

Chapter 5: 54
1975-76: *Wings Over The World*

Chapter 6: 60
1976-79: *Wings Over New Waves*

Chapter 7: 68
1979-86: *War And Peace*

Chapter 8: 82
1987-93: *Animals, Elvis And Classical Gas*

Chapter 9: 88
1993-99: *Fireman With An Hourglass*

Chapter 10: 94
1999-2003: *Hatches, Matches, Dispatches*

Epilogue: 98
2003-2023: *Chaos And Creation*

Biographies 106

Discography 124

Studio Albums / Live Albums / Soundtracks,
Covers, Curiosities / Compilations / Boxsets /
Classical Albums / Ambient, Electronic, Mash-
Up, Remix Albums / 50 Highest Ranking Singles

Acknowledgements And Sources 188

Introduction

Anyone foolish enough to take on writing a book about Paul McCartney's solo career, even one as relatively succinct as this illustrated overview, should be forewarned and reminded that he, the world's most successful ever songwriter and popular musician, has been around... almost forever.

The Beatles were formed in 1960 and entertained the world incomparably for the next 10 years. When they unofficially broke-up in 1970, McCartney was 28 years of age; by the time this book is published, he'll be 81. From the day the Beatles ceased to be, for more than 50 years he has never stopped working. And what has he achieved? What hasn't he? Rock, pop, rock 'n' roll, jazz, soul, disco, film music, TV themes, easy listening, electronic, techno, orchestral, ballet, baroque, oratorios, rap, music hall parodies, songs for crooners and even a few children's ditties. As *Rolling Stone* magazine commented when celebrating his 60 years in the music business: "Make a list of all the songwriters who were composing great tunes in 1958. Now make an overlapping list of the ones who are still writing brilliant songs in 2018. Your list reads: Paul McCartney."

Such an unprecedented back-catalogue partially explains why, for some peculiar reason, not everyone has taken McCartney very seriously since the Beatles split, or liked him very much because "it was all his fault". In reality, each of the Fab Four played their role in the band's four-way divorce; equally, few fans over a certain age would claim Paul's (or John, George or Ringo's) solo material compares well to the Beatles' staggeringly brilliant 10-year canon of work. It is the benchmark against which every McCartney song since 1970 has been measured. One of the pleasures of putting this book together has been the experience of playing just about everything he's produced over the last 50-odd years - some for the first time. It would be a lie to claim I enjoyed everything (there are one or two... unusual... aspects among Paul's overall output, just as there were within the Beatles'), but it also includes some of the best material of his entire career.

Good, bad or indifferent, McCartney has had to deal with elements of severe criticism and hysterical praise from the public, media and his devoted fan base during that period; most performers would have struggled to cope with such intensity at either end of the scale. Add to that his own problems with nervous breakdowns, disagreements with bandmates, world-famous drug busts, personal tragedy and marital nightmares, McCartney's career has certainly been a (very) long and winding road. Despite unprecedented success resulting in a bulging bank account and properties around the world, McCartney has done his best to maintain a 'normal' life for himself and, perhaps more importantly, for his family. In proving there was life beyond the Beatles he sustained a level of sanity most would have found impossible.

"That is the funny thing about fame," he says, "you sort of look in the mirror and just think, 'Oh, I am the guy I've read so much about.' But I try and disassociate myself from him a bit. I try and be the kid I was when I was five, growing up. Paul McCartney is the sort of successful bit of it all, that I'm very proud of, but I daren't imagine I'm him. Cause it'd just blow my head off."

From the Beatles in the Sixties, Wings in the Seventies and a successful solo career throughout the Eighties and beyond, he's done a pretty good job at getting inside our heads with some of the greatest popular music ever written. Just another day for Paul McCartney.

Pete Chrisp June 2023

'...Oh, I am the guy I've read so much about.'
Paul McCartney

Prologue
1967-69: The Beginning Of The End

1969. A very important year in the history of popular music, possibly even rock 'n' roll's greatest year, for so many valid reasons. Think about it.

Arguably 1969 saw the release of the word's first ever rock opera from the Who, the brilliant *Tommy*, which they performed live at two of the biggest festivals of all time – Bob Dylan and the Band at the Isle of Wight... and Woodstock – a miraculous 4-day event that climaxed with Jimi Hendrix's earth-shattering performance at 9am on a Monday morning in front of less than 10 per cent of the weekend's audience of more than half a million. Those who didn't wait that long had already seen some amazing bands from relatively new names such as Crosby, Stills, Nash and Young, Santana, Ten Years After and Joe Cocker, all of whom would go on to garner worldwide success as a result.

It was the year Led Zeppelin released their first two albums, Deep Purple their eponymous third, and Black Sabbath were in the process of recording their self-titled debut with the result of rock music being transformed into something so much louder, more aggressive, and more exciting forever. Plenty of other influential debut LPs arrived in 1969 from the likes of the Stooges, the Allman Brothers and MC5's *Kick Out the Jams*. The world's great soul singers gave us such masterworks as Dusty Springfield's stunning LP, *Dusty in Memphis*, while Isaac Hayes produced his landmark album *Hot Buttered Soul* and funk maestros Sly and the Family Stone released their controversial *Stand!* just a few weeks before performing it to great acclaim at Woodstock.

Folk music certainly wasn't standing still, with the arrival of Nick Drake's superb *Five Years Left* and Fairport Convention's hugely influential folk-rock album, *Liege and Lief*. In the world of modern jazz Miles Davis revealed his first jazz-fusion album, *In a Silent Way*, followed just a few months later by Frank Zappa's mind-blowingly jazz-influenced *Hot Rats*. And the world was introduced to a brand new happy sound from Jamaica with the release of Desmond Dekker and the Ace's 'Israelites', a worldwide Top 10 hit and the UK's first reggae No. 1.

Nothing in the world of popular music would ever be quite the same again, but sadly not everything in 1969 represented peace and love. The Rolling Stones brought out *Let it Bleed* in November '69 with an album cover portraying a cake in the form of discs stacked on a record player. It was the unknown Delia Smith who made the cake. The year had not been easy for the Stones when founder member Brian Jones was kicked out of the band due to his problems with drugs and drink. Mick Taylor replaced him just a few weeks before Jones was found dead in his swimming pool under suspicious circumstances. Two days after his death, on 5 July 1969, the Stones decided to go ahead with their free concert at London's Hyde Park in tribute to Brian, supported by the world's first genuinely prog-rock band, King Crimson. UK Hells Angels were employed to handle show security at the concert, with nothing too serious taking place, but the

Right: Press Launch for 'Sergeant Pepper's Lonely Hearts Club Band', held at Brian Epstein's house at 24 Chapel Street, London, 19th May 1967

Stones' management then made the mistake of hiring US Hells Angels again in December 1969 for a free concert at the Altamont Speedway in California. The result was an 18-year-old black man being murdered in front of the stage as the Stones performed 'Sympathy for the Devil' just a few feet away. Although not to blame, neither was it the band's finest hour.

The Stones main rivals, and friends, of course, were the Beatles, who in 1969 responded to myriad internal and external issues by writing, recording and, in September of that glorious year, releasing what many now regard as their greatest ever album, *Abbey Road*. They were the Beatles and *Abbey Road* represented 1969's cream on the cake. During their nine years together from 1960 to 1969, the last two years had been nothing short of triumphant. After 1966's stunning *Revolver* followed by earth-shattering *Sgt. Pepper's Lonely Hearts Club Band* and *The Beatles* (or 'White Album') and now, in 1969, yet another masterpiece, *Abbey Road*. As 1970 loomed and the explosion of new Beatles-influenced music prepared to take to the stage, nothing, it seemed, could go wrong. But it did. Even in the greatest times, people make bad mistakes. With that much talent bursting at the scenes, it was inevitable.

When, and why, exactly, did the Beatles fall apart? There is a sequence of five major factors that brought about the downfall of the world's greatest ever band. First, in 1967 the Beatles released *Sgt. Pepper's Lonely Hearts Club Band*, the LP against which all other albums before and since tend to be measured, having sat at the top of virtually every 'Greatest Albums of All Time' polls for 30 years. The album sold in bucketloads and went straight to No. 1 almost immediately around the world, holding that position for months. Undoubtedly *Sgt. Pepper* changed the way people listened to and appreciated popular music but also changed the way in which the Beatles themselves viewed their future together. It made all four of them an absolute fortune, but with that came new issues, responsibilities and disagreements. In effect, they became victims of their own success.

Following the second world war, income tax rates in the Fifties and Sixties in the UK had risen at its highest level to more than 90% and the Beatles' manager Brian Epstein had come up with a plan to lower their personal tax bills. He would invest £2m of excess profits into a new business venture to replace the existing Beatles Ltd; if he didn't, the money would be handed over to the Inland Revenue.

An executive board including Brian Epstein, his personal assistant Alistair Taylor, the band's road manager Neil Aspinall and various accountants and lawyers came up with ideas to create new Beatles merchandising shops; the band members all agreed that was incredibly tedious. Together they decided to get involved and come up with some more inspirational suggestions as to how they should spend and invest this money. The first of those five major factors: A is for Apple.

It was McCartney who came up with the name 'Apple', according to the band's press officer and publicist Derek Taylor, when Paul visited his London flat one day. He said, "We're starting a brand new form of business. So, what is the first thing that a child is taught when he begins to grow up? A is for Apple." Paul actually wanted to add the word 'Core' to the business title, as a joke, but in the end the word 'Corps' (an American military or business term with the same pronunciation) was acceptable and actually more amusing.

The four Beatles had come up with the concept of Apple Corps as a new business conglomerate of which the chief element would be Apple Records plus several other divisions representing some of their own personal interests, including Apple Electronics, Apple Films, Apple Publishing and Apple Retail, most notably what would eventually become a short-lived Apple Boutique on central London's Baker Street with the company HQ on the upper floors. "An Aladdin's cave of music and art'" as the broadcast media described it.

Everything was looking very promising and, on 25 August 1967, as part of this happy all-togetherness that the band

Prologue: 1967-69: The Beginning Of The End

seemed to be experiencing at the time, and having recently discovered their own interest in Indian culture, three of the Beatles with their wives and partners (not Ringo, whose wife Maureen had just given birth) all boarded a train to Bangor in north Wales to attend a seminar on Transcendental Meditation hosted by Indian teacher Maharishi Mahesh Yogi. All found the course fascinating and had expressed interest in visiting India to study TM in more depth... when dreadful news arrived: Brian Epstein had been found dead at his home in London as the result of an accidental overdose of barbiturates. Major factor number two: E is for Epstein.

Four days later, with their captain gone and the Beatles cruise ship rudderless, the band members met at Paul's house in London to discuss what they should do. It was Paul who took responsibility for steering them in the right direction by convincing the others that the best thing to do was just carry on; they should get underway with the Beatles' first Apple Films project, *Magical Mystery Tour*. Without Epstein there to offer any guidance, or even question such questionable concepts, Paul's loose idea for a TV movie of a psychedelic, multi-coloured bus trundling around England's country lanes proved a mistake. Broadcast by the BBC on Boxing Day 1967 (in black and white!), it wasn't well-received by the public or media and became the Beatles' first major disappointment – just seven months after *Sgt. Pepper* had ruled the world. Thankfully it didn't ruin Paul's Christmas too much; the day before, on Christmas Day, he and his girlfriend, actress Jane Asher, had announced their engagement to be married.

In February 1968, to continue their studies of TM and Indian culture, the Beatles (this time all four, again with wives and partner) headed over to Rishikesh in India to spend almost two months meditating with Maharishi Mahesh Yogi and chill out away from the media mayhem of recent months. They also used the time to write more than 30 numbers, of which 17 would eventually appear on the 'White Album'. A perfect result, it seemed, but beneath the calm TM façade, serious cracks were beginning to appear. Ringo and his wife Maureen

were the first to leave India after two weeks because they hated the food and insects constantly buzzing around. McCartney and his fiancé Jane Asher departed in mid-March claiming they had other work commitments, although it appears their engagement announcement three months earlier had created problems; McCartney was one of the most desired and sought after men in the world and was seriously questioning himself as to whether he wanted to give up such freedom.

Similarly, John Lennon and George Harrison and their wives stuck it out almost to the end of the TM course, but John left primarily because he was missing the woman he had met at a London art gallery and fallen in love with in 1966 – Japanese artist and musician Yoko Ono. It was in India that John decided his loveless marriage to his wife Cynthia must come to an end; once back in London, John and Yoko's relationship deepened in May of that year and, within six months, he and Cynthia were divorced. Major factor number three: O is for Ono.

Despite their various personal and professional problems, Apple Corps had continued to blossom as a creative outlet for the Beatles to introduce new artists, including some notable successes signed within the first year: American folk singer James Taylor, for example, and UK TV's *Opportunity Knocks* talent show winner, Mary Hopkin, a teenage girl from Wales who McCartney took under his wing to help launch her career.

By May 1968 Apple had progressed sufficiently for Paul and John to fly out to New York to announce their new business venture and hold a press conference at the Americana Hotel to explain what the concept of Apple was all about. Paul described it as being "controlled weirdness... a kind of western communism" and went on to say, "if you come to see me and say 'I've had such and such a dream', I'll say, 'Here's so much money. Go away and do it.' We've already bought all our dreams. So now we want to share that possibility with others." Apple accountants may well have felt slight twitches of concern when hearing the use of such phrases as "so much money", but the concept went down well in America

and made the trip to New York well-worth the effort; for Paul, there was an even better reason for the visit, which would prove hugely important over the next 30 years.

Back in May 1967, just as *Sgt. Pepper* was about to be launched, Paul had gone out one evening to the well-known London music venue, the Bag O'Nails, with three of the Beatles' inner circle: roadie Mal Evans, tour manager Neil Aspinall and Brian Epstein's other personal assistant Peter Brown. They spent the night watching Georgie Fame perform with his band, and it was there for the first time Paul spotted a young woman he instantly found very interesting. She was an American photographer called Linda Eastman who, back in New York, by sheer perseverance, had become the unofficial Fillmore East concert hall staff photographer, gaining access to just about everybody, from Jimi Hendrix and the Doors to the Who and Bob Dylan. In 1967 she had won the 'US Female Photographer of the Year' award and, with a growing reputation, was invited to England on assignment to take pictures for a book in progress called *Rock and Other Four-Letter Words: Music of the Electric Generation*, by the US writer J. Marks.

Linda was sitting at a table with the English band the Animals and Scottish singer Lulu; when the show finished and they all

Above: Linda Eastman talks to Paul McCartney at the press launch of 'Sergeant Pepper's Lonely Hearts Club Band'

Right: Linda Eastman, in London, Dec 1968

got up to leave, Paul skillfully "stood up just as she was passing, blocking her exit. And so I said, 'Oh, sorry. Hi. How are you? How're you doing?' I introduced myself, and said, 'We're going on to another club after this, would you like to join us?' That was my big pulling line!" They all headed to the Speakeasy club just up the road in Soho, and later back to Paul's house in Cavendish Avenue, St John's Wood, for a few drinks.

Peter Brown (who remembers the evening differently and claims he introduced Paul to Linda) had been impressed by Linda's pictures and invited her to attend the launch party for *Sgt. Pepper* four days later at Brian's Epstein's London home – an opportunity to get some terrific shots. After she left the party, Paul would not see Linda again for another year. When he and John Lennon visited New York to launch Apple in 1968, Linda attended the press conference at the Americana Hotel and was invited to travel to the airport with them the following day to spend some time with Paul. He returned to the USA shortly afterwards for more Apple promotion work in California and left Linda a message as to where she could find him. The next day she arrived at his hotel having flown from New York and their relationship went to the next level.

In July, Jane Asher called off her engagement to Paul, not because of Linda but as a result of returning home to London unexpectedly one day to catch Paul in bed with a girl called Francie Schwartz, a New York film-maker who had approached Apple for finance and ended up with more than she bargained for – including a job in Derek Taylor's press office. Paul was proving himself to be one of London's busiest men about town. The affair with Schwartz had continued after his first night with Linda in California; when he subsequently phoned Linda to invite her over to stay with him in London, he was actually on holiday in Sardinia with another former girlfriend, a model called Maggie McGivern, who he'd been having an affair with since 1966.

Linda had previously been married for three years to an old college boyfriend called Joseph Melville See Jr., known as

Mel, with whom she had a daughter, Heather, now almost six years old. Coming over to London with a young child wasn't that easy but she agreed to pay a visit in September 1968, leaving Heather behind in New York cared for by her family.

In Abbey Road Studios with the Beatles working hard on what it had been decided would be a double album, *The Beatles*, it was soon increasingly clear they were all starting to get on each other's nerves, now with two new strong-minded women to add to the cauldron. John and Yoko had become so devoted to one another that Yoko was now sitting-in on almost every recording session, quite literally, right next to him on a stool. It was now Yoko he would turn to for advice about

his voice or guitar, not the other Beatles, even though she knew little about pop music. The tiniest of things began to make life difficult for the others – helping herself to George Harrison's digestive biscuits, for example, without so much as a by-your-leave!

The pinnacle was when Yoko (pregnant at the time) was told by doctors she needed lots of bed rest following a car accident while on holiday in Scotland. The vast majority of people would have sensibly stayed at home. Not Yoko. She asked John to order a bed from Harrods and have it delivered to the studio. Above the bed he attached a microphone so that she could communicate with the band whenever she felt it necessary. For the other three Beatles, it was the day the word 'gobsmacked' was invented. The overall feeling within the previously tight studio environment rapidly deteriorated. In a cold, fragmented atmosphere, arguments between the band simmered. Even their calm and reliable producer, George Martin, decided half way through the sessions that he needed a holiday: "It was a tough time, really tough," he said. "They were so much at each other's throats."

Truth was, nobody was having much fun and *The Beatles* album ceased to be a band project; at times the three main songwriters would be recording in three different studios, with Ringo flitting between them or, at times, sitting bored to tears in the studio's reception. No surprise that early in the sessions he decided he'd had enough and quit the band. It was almost three weeks before his bandmates persuaded him to return.

Right: Paul McCartney puts a protective arm around his wife Linda as they make their way through the crowds gathered outside Marylebone Registry Office on their wedding day. 12th March 1969

Just as John was now besotted with Yoko, Paul began to realise, after a few days of Linda being around the house, that she meant much more to him than a succession of young women prancing around at any time of the day or night. Francie Schwartz had been sent packing but Paul urgently needed someone else to help sort out his life. When Linda arrived in September she had been shocked at what a sloppy bachelor pad his London home had turned into and devoted considerable time tidying up his mess for him. Paul soon appreciated the fact that his life was much more fun, and cleaner, with Linda Eastman about the place.

Once the 'White Album' was completed in October 1968, Paul and Linda returned to New York not only for him to meet Linda's daughter Heather for the first time, but also Linda's parents and brother, with whom he got on very well. Both Linda's father, Lee, and her brother, John, were entertainment lawyers with considerable experience in the music business – which must have crossed Paul's mind as being something possibly quite useful in the near future…

For the next few days Paul, Linda and Heather spent time together strolling around the streets of New York wearing scruffy old clothes, Paul unshaven, in an effort not to be recognised or bothered, which largely they weren't. He loved every minute – this was a new experience for him, wandering the Big Apple soaking-in its many cultural opportunities. Linda, through her family and music contacts, could open just about any door and it was there that Paul met well-known artists and writers, paid a visit to see Bob Dylan again and attended concerts at jazz clubs and at the Fillmore East and Apollo in Harlem. He visited museums and art galleries and was hugely impressed by Lee Eastman's own art collection, some on display at home: Picasso, Matisse and a huge collection of paintings and sculptures by Willem de Kooning.

Very impressive, but Paul was moved even more by the way Linda looked after her daughter so lovingly and was such an obviously natural mother. After that short period in

New York it was time to return to London, but this time with Heather in tow, and talk of wedding bells already in the air. A few days later they made the journey up to Scotland to spend some time in a rather dilapidated old farm building on almost 200 acres of land that Paul had bought back in June 1966 with help from Jane Asher. High Park Farm up in Campbeltown, near the Mull of Kintyre, was purchased partly as an investment to reduce his income tax bill but was also a place in the middle of nowhere (not even the middle!) that could provide sanctuary away from the crazy world of the Beatles. Paul was concerned Linda and Heather might hate it and want to return to London immediately. Luckily, both loved it. No hot water, hardly any furniture, and a few rats here and there… but the space, the silence, the isolation, the freedom, the farm animals… Perfect. "We could do this place up… I could make a nice home here," said Linda. Little did she know how important that would prove.

The new McCartney family returned to their London home together, this time for good. In December that year, while on a holiday in Portugal, Paul proposed to Linda, who by then was pregnant with their first child together, Mary. They were married at Marylebone Registry Office in London on 12 March 1969.

None of the other Beatles attended.

Chapter 1
1969-70: The End

In January 1969, three months after the Beatles had finished the 'White Album', rehearsals got underway at Twickenham Film Studios as part of Paul McCartney's concept for a 'behind the scenes' TV documentary on the band preparing to perform live in a series of concerts at the Roundhouse in north London. It was McCartney's attempt to rekindle everyone's enthusiasm once again in being a simple, but rather brilliant, rock 'n' roll band, just as they had been back in 1960 when they set out on their adventure. In reality, it proved to be little more than a pipedream.

The filmed rehearsals, originally known as the 'Get Back' sessions, were sometimes soured by an environment of arguments and ill-feeling, resulting in Harrison walking out on 10 January and announcing he was leaving the Beatles. A week later his bandmates managed to woo him back by agreeing to record at the brand new and better equipped Apple Studios at the company's new offices in Savile Row, central London, where they had moved a few months earlier.

Things weren't helped during that difficult week when John Lennon, concerned about the amount of money being syphoned by some of Apple Corps' wacky investments and wasted by some of the staff's extravagant spending habits, spoke to *Disc and Music Echo* magazine's Ray Coleman, who

Right: Paul McCartney leaving Apple Headquarters in his 1965 Mini Cooper, 19th April 1969

Chapter 1: 1969-70: *The End*   19

printed the story on 13 January. Said John: "We haven't got half the money people think we have. We have enough to live on, but we can't let Apple go on like it is. We started off with loads of ideas of what we wanted to do... but, like one or two Beatles things, it didn't work out because we weren't quick enough to realise that we needed a businessman's brain to run the whole thing. Apple's losing money every week because it needs closely running by a big businessman... It's got to be a business first... It needs a broom and a lot of people there will have to go. It needs streamlining. It doesn't need to make vast profits, but if it carries on like this, all of us will be broke in the next six months."

Among the many millions who raised their eyebrows at such surprising news was Allen Klein, a tough-talking American music business executive currently managing the Rolling Stones. Klein had expressed an interest in the Beatles as far back as 1964 when he tried to sign them to RCA Records, but Brian Epstein had refused. After reading Lennon's interview, Klein contacted the Beatles' press officer Derek Taylor, who passed him on to Peter Brown, who gave him John's phone number and a meeting was arranged for Monday 27 January at the Dorchester Hotel in London. Both John and Yoko were impressed by Klein's straight-talking (particularly Yoko, when he claimed he could organise an art exhibition for her) and immediately retained him to represent them financially. The next day John introduced Klein to the other three Beatles. Major factor number four: K is for Klein.

Chapter 1: 1969-70: *The End*   21

Paul, of course, had also been concerned for some time as to what was happening at Apple and had spoken to his soon-to-be father in law, Lee Eastman, and brother-in-law John to see if they would be interested in taking control of the Beatles' finances. Lee thought his son John would be perfect for the role. When Paul suggested this to the others, however, John, George and Ringo made it clear their preference was for Klein. As Lennon put it: "John Eastman gave me the impression of being an inexperienced, somewhat excitable and easily confused young man. We all knew of Paul's friendship with the family... I was against the idea of having, as manager, anyone in such a close relationship with any particular Beatle, but, apart from that, they did not strike us as having the right experience or knowledge for the job."

Paul, conversely, had serious doubts about Klein; the Eastmans had informed him that Klein had pending legal issues with the US tax authorities; on top of that, Mick Jagger contacted Paul to let him know the Rolling Stones were trying to offload Klein as their manager as they'd discovered he was "a crook". Nevertheless, at the other three's insistence, an agreement was reached that Klein would be the Beatles' interim manager while the Eastmans would act as their lawyers for a short period. Klein moved in to the Apple offices to investigate the company's financial situation and in a short space of time

Paul McCartney, Ringo Starr, John Lennon and George Harrison, attend an Apple Corps meeting circa 1969

had sacked most of the staff, even trying to dismiss some of the inner circle including Neil Aspinall, but the Beatles all agreed that was unacceptable. Some of Apple's major stars couldn't wait to get away once Klein was on the scene, including James Taylor who was now managed by Jane Asher's brother, Peter. Again the band were at least decent enough to release him from his contract without any ridiculous extraction charges Klein would have imposed on them.

The new atmosphere at Apple was far away from the slaphappy business approach that had been deemed essential when the company was created; Klein's negativity began to have an effect on everyone, including the band. The final straw came on 9 May 1969 when the Beatles were meant to have a recording session at Olympia Studio in west London but it dissolved into a massive argument. Klein insisted they all had to sign his three-year management contract that evening before he returned to New York the next day. Paul, very unhappy with Klein's insistence on 20 per cent of everything, even income from work before he arrived on the scene, refused to sign it. The other three Beatles stormed out of the studio leaving Paul all alone and feeling very sore. He never did sign the contract.

Linda McCartney summed it all up: "It was weird times. Allen Klein was stirring it up something awful. Between Allen Klein in one ear and Yoko in the other ear, they had John so spinning about Paul it was really quite heartbreaking."

Top Right: John Lennon and Yoko Ono with their manager Allen Klein in 1969

Bottom Right: The famous 'Abbey Road' cover

K is for Klein. O is for Ono. Two major factors combine. Knockout.

In September 1969, the band gathered at Apple to sign a new contract with Capitol Records, who had agreed, after heavy negotiations with Klein, to increase their US royalties to an unprecedented 25 per cent. Even Paul had to agree that was good work and, in the spirit of the moment, tried once again to convince the other three that they could resolve any issues between themselves, maybe even get back on the road and start playing smaller venues again, like they used to back in the early days. They could use a pseudonym so fans wouldn't know in advance... John was incredulous. "I think you're daft," he said. "Klein asked me not to tell you but, seeing as you asked me, I'm leaving the group. I want a divorce, like my divorce from Cynthia."

Ironic, given that six months earlier, on 20 March (just 10 days after Paul's marriage to Linda), John had taken Yoko to Gibraltar where local laws allowed them to get married at short notice. Once hitched, they flew to Amsterdam and performed their famous weeklong bed-in supporting world peace and protesting against the Vietnam War. Paul and Linda, on their own honeymoon in New York, watched it all in amazement on television. These were now two very different men, different wives, different couples. As Paul put it: "He'd met Yoko and I don't think he wanted to play with his little play-friends anymore. I did."

The day before John and Yoko's meeting with Klein at the Dorchester, someone at Apple had come up with the brainwave of the Beatles playing a live concert – not at the Roundhouse, but on the roof of the Apple building in Savile Row. This, they decided, would be the perfect climax for the 'Get Back' sessions, which had now been elevated to the status of a proper movie, not just a TV documentary. On Thursday 30 January at around

Chapter 1: 1969-70: *The End*   23

lunchtime, the band headed to the roof to perform. After 42 minutes the celebrated concert was curtailed by the Metropolitan Police, and the Beatles' final live performance was at an end. Once over, any enthusiasm for the 'Get Back' sessions had gone; the only positive was the release of 'Get Back' as a single on 11 April 1969. The remaining recordings were shelved and the band began work on their swansong, *Abbey Road*.

On 14 April John and Paul had gone into Abbey Road Studio with George Martin to record the single 'The Ballad of John and Yoko', a humorous if somewhat bitter account of the couple's wedding in March. With neither Ringo or George available, and John wanting to get the single released as quickly as possible while his bedroom activities in Amsterdam were still hot news, it was down to him and McCartney to work together for a whole day. It didn't bode well, given the anguish of recent months, but they seemed to enjoy themselves. As sound engineer Geoff Emerick described it in his autobiography, "They reverted to being two old school chums, all the nastiness of recent months swept under the rug and replaced by the sheer joy of making music together."

It was the last time John and Paul would play like that together. Despite the brilliance and huge success of *Abbey Road* released in September that year, the Beatles now had nothing more to offer apart from some rough tapes of the 'Get Back' sessions that nobody liked very much. The recordings were initially handed over to producer Glyn Johns in an effort to make something of them; he did his best but, once completed, the tapes were shelved, where they gathered dust for nine months. Paul was feeling very much the same.

Once *Abbey Road* was finished, it seemed the four Beatles didn't want to spend any time together at all. Their final photo session for the US compilation album *Hey Jude* took place at John's home in Tittenhurst, Surrey, on 22 August 1969, with Linda McCartney capturing the images of their dark clothes, awkward stances and tired faces as if all were attending the funeral of someone close. In effect, they were.

Once done they all headed to their homes and closed the shutters, except Paul, who immediately headed up to High Park Farm in Scotland with his family to consider his future. "We took the kids, we took the dogs, we took everything we had, a guitar on top and a potty for the baby." In effect, he disappeared – so much so that rumours began to spread around the world that Paul was dead. He certainly wasn't in a great frame of mind – his mental health was at an all time low while his use of drugs

Chapter 1: 1969-70: *The End*   25

Perched on the bumper of their Land-Rover at their remote Scottish family farm, Paul, wife Linda, Linda's daughter Heather and 2-month-old Mary McCartney—posed for a picture to reassure Paul's fans of his well-being.

Safe in his very own Scotland yard

and whisky was at an all-time high. He was suffering from a nervous breakdown. Without Linda and his children there to help him through these dark days, who knows what might have happened?

He was, he said, "...just living in a cloud and the mist rolling in from the sea and just trying to figure out what I could do, you know, but it wasn't clear for a few months... I felt my life was over. I thought, I'm not worth anything anymore. I was fairly wiped out. For the first time in my life I was on the scrapheap."

When America's *Life* magazine tracked him down and sent over a writer and photographer to get a scoop, Paul was furious and threw a bucket of kitchen waste at them, which the photographer caught on film. It wasn't the kind of thing Paul would normally do and he soon apologised, agreeing to an interview if they spiked that aspect of the day's events. "Perhaps the ['Paul is dead'] rumour started because I haven't been in the press much lately. I have done enough press for a lifetime and I don't have anything to say these days."

He did, of course: "The Beatle thing is over. It has been exploded." Nobody at that stage knew that John was leaving the Beatles, and yet Paul's comment seemed to go unnoticed, as if he didn't mean it. But he did. Linda calmed him down and reassured him this wasn't the end; he could make music all by himself, without the other Beatles. With her love and support he began to realise he couldn't carry on like this anymore. He needed to go home, back to London, and start working on something for himself. His first solo album.

Opp. Page: The Beatles performing their last live public concert on the rooftop of the Apple building in London's Savile Row, 30th January 1969

Above Left & Right: Life Magazine's revealing 1969 interview with Paul in Scotland

Chapter 2:
1970-71: The New Beginning

Shortly before Christmas 1969 Paul and his family returned to Cavendish Avenue in London to get back to work. He'd already been tinkering with a few songs up in Scotland and also had plenty of numbers intended for the Beatles that had never made it onto any of the albums. Once home, with help from one of the Abbey Road sound engineers, he installed a four-track recording machine and, surrounded by instruments he would play all by himself, started putting down some ideas on tape. In the process of making sure the recorder was working ok, the first thing he laid down was a snippet of an acoustic number made up of little more than the words, 'The Lovely Linda'. It wasn't much but meant a lot to him and became the first track on *McCartney*.

Getting the album eventually released, however, would involve many more boardroom battles between Paul, the Beatles and Allen Klein. Back in 1967 when Apple was formed, all four of the Beatles had signed a contract that bound them together financially for 10 years. What it meant was that any solo projects – such as John's weird *Unfinished Music* and *Wedding Album* with Yoko, Ringo's *Sentimental Journey* and George's *Wonderwall Music* (all of which were released before *McCartney*) would all be shared equally. Paul wasn't happy with that situation; none of those albums had sold very well and it wasn't his fault that the Beatles were over; he just wanted his independence. But he was trapped – Klein and the other three Beatles refused to release him from Apple.

When Paul tried to reason with George Harrison one

day, his response was, "You'll stay on the fucking label! Hare Krishna." Once again the situation started to have a negative impact on Paul's frame of mind, causing nightmares about Klein's level of control; would he ever be able to escape from his grasp? It's not only dreams that come true – sometimes nightmares do as well.

With his solo album recorded at home and mixed at Abbey Road and Morgan Studios in London, Paul had contacted Neil Aspinall at Apple to arrange a release date, which was penciled in for 17 April. In January 1970 Lennon had been working on his third solo single, 'Instant Karma' with American record producer Phil Spector, famous for his 'Wall of Sound' bells and whistles approach to recording. So impressed was he with Spector's work that, without consulting any of his bandmates, Lennon handed over the 'Get Back" session tapes that had been gathering dust on the shelf for nine months. His instructions were to make something from what he described as "the shittiest load of badly recorded shit".

When Spector's work on the album (now under the title *Let it Be*) was presented to the band, John loved it, George Harrison and Ringo weren't too concerned, but original producer George Martin was far from happy. And McCartney was livid, especially with his song 'The Long and Winding

Right: Paul and Linda McCartney at their High Park Farm near Campbeltown, Scotland, with their dog Martha, February 1971

Chapter 2: 1970-71: The New Beginning   27

Road', which he felt had been ruined by Spector's orchestral and choral overdubs. He did his best to stop the album being released, but Klein was never going to allow that to happen. Major breakup factor number five. L is for *Let it Be*.

As George Martin commented in the Beatles' *Anthology* book: "That made me angry – and it made Paul even angrier, because neither he nor I knew about it until it had been done. It happened behind our backs because it was done when Allen Klein was running John. He'd organised Phil Spector and I think George and Ringo had gone along with it."

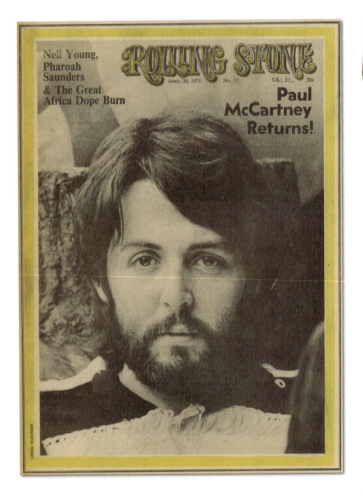

Worse was to come when Paul received a letter from Lennon and Harrison, under instructions from Klein, that *Let it Be* was planned for release on 28 April, and Ringo's solo album *Sentimental Journey* on 27 March, therefore *McCartney* would be postponed until 4 June. Bravely, thinking he was doing the decent thing, Ringo actually delivered the letter to Paul by hand, and was rapidly thrown out of Paul's house with his ears ringing. For Paul this was the straw that broke the camel's back. Although the other Beatles eventually backed down and allowed *McCartney* to be released on 17 April, the fuse had been lit.

Above: Rear cover of Paul's first solo album 'McCartney'

Left: Rolling Stone magazine front cover, 1970

To avoid any need for a press conference to promote the release of *McCartney*, which he didn't feel capable of handling, Paul, with the help of Apple's Derek Taylor and Peter Brown, put together a lengthy Question and Answer package for delivery to the media on 9 April, which included some interesting pointers as to his and the Beatles' future:

Q: Is this album a rest away from the Beatles or the start of a solo career?

A: Time will tell. Being a solo album means it's the start of a solo career... and not being done with the Beatles means it's a rest. So it's both.

Q: Is your break from the Beatles temporary or permanent, due to personal difference or musical ones?

A: Personal differences, business differences, musical differences, but most of all because I have a better time with my family. Temporary or permanent? I don't know.

Q: Do you see a time when Lennon-McCartney becomes an active songwriting partnership again?

A: No.

No surprise that headlines appeared the next day with the first from the *Daily Mirror*: "PAUL IS QUITTING THE BEATLES", followed by twisted variations around the world along the lines of: "PAUL BREAKS UP THE BEATLES." While trying to do the right thing, Paul had been basically thrown under the bus. Even young girls hanging around Cavendish Avenue now hated Paul McCartney, despite the fact that he was the last of the four to quit at some stage, but nobody knew about that.

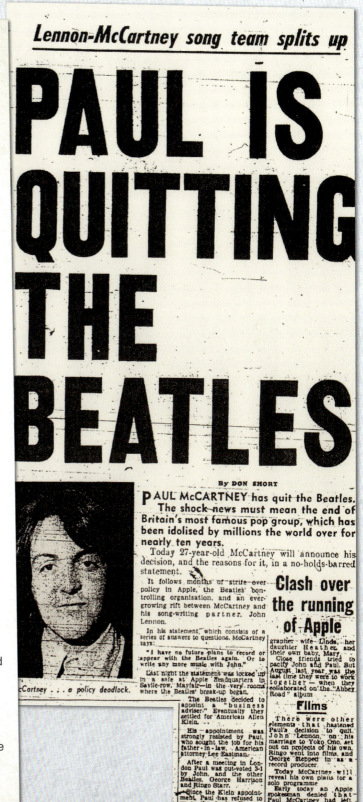

an intimate bioscopic experience with
THE BEATLES

APPLE
An **abkco** managed company
presents

"Let it be"

The final, *final* straw was when *Let it Be* was released on 8 May 1970 with none of Paul's requests for changes (in a letter he'd written to Klein) having been implemented; Klein didn't even respond. Paul spoke to Lee Eastman about the possibility of suing Klein but was advised against it. His best option, said Eastman, was to sue John, George and Ringo and breakup the Beatles. Paul was traumatised by the very thought of it but eventually realised he had no other choice: "...these truest friends of mine were now my firmest enemies overnight. I knew I had to do it. It was either that or letting Klein have the whole thing, all the fortune we'd worked for all our lives since we were children." Eastman also suggested that Paul should buy up more shares in Northern Songs, the Beatles music publishing company, to give himself more bargaining power in any future negotiations. Paul gave his lawyers the go-ahead and let them get on with putting the case together over the next six months while he concentrated on returning to what he loved best – making music.

BELOW: Beatles fans stage a protest march on hearing Paul McCartney is leaving the Beatles. April 29, 1970, Tokyo, Japan

LEFT: A poster for the Apple Corps movie 'Let It Be', released 20 May, 1970

McCartney sold well in both the UK and USA but wasn't particularly well-received by the media, many of whom found it too raw, with too many rough edges and instrumental fillers. It was disappointing for Paul and there was no doubt some critics were dipping their pens in vitriol as a result of claims he had caused the Beatles' breakup. Things didn't improve a week later when the film *Let it Be* was released in cinemas to equally mediocre reviews; critics, unsurprisingly, focused on the brief argument between Paul and George as if here was the evidence that McCartney was a tyrant attempting to take over the band, if not the world. (Disney's documentary *The Beatles: Get Back* released in 2021 includes eight hours of the 'Get Back' sessions at Twickenham Film Studios and clearly demonstrates that, in reality, they all got on pretty well most of the time.)

The answer, Paul decided, after a summer break in Scotland with his family, was to head over to New York in October 1970 to work on another album, this time with Linda as co-writer and performer, and with other musicians to provide the depth, intensity and professionalism that some critics felt were lacking from *McCartney*. Without revealing who the sessions were for, he organised auditions at an old basement studio in central New York, threw out the bait and waiting to see what he might catch. One of the first to bite was a 27-year-old drummer, Denny Seiwell – the first future member of an, as yet, unnamed or even thought about band. Further auditions with guitarists found a session player called David Spinozza, and work began.

Linda made a contribution to the writing of six of the numbers on the as yet untitled album as well as backing vocals, which, although far from being a professional musician, she handled very well. The only problem that occurred as recording continued was that, being used to having musicians available whenever he needed them, Paul found it hard to accept that session players often have other commitments and couldn't drop everything if he clicked his fingers. David Spinozza, much in demand, was eventually dropped for that reason and replaced by Hugh McCracken. By November, most of the album had been put together and the McCartneys returned to the UK.

On 15 November 1970, through his solicitors, Paul filed his lawsuit against the other Beatles and Apple Corps in the High Courts of London. On 31 December 1970 the papers were delivered to John, George, Ringo and Apple seeking to end the Beatles and the company. The lawsuit also requested that a receiver should be appointed for Apple to freeze their assets until the case had been settled, and that Allen Klein should be charged with mismanagement of the Apple funds. And a Happy New Year to you, too. As far as Paul was concerned, there was evidence that Klein had been ripping off the Rolling Stones, and the Beatles were his next target. "It was really painful," said Paul, "but I had to take a stand."

It was not a happy time for anyone. Paul's former bandmates were shocked and angered by what he had done and furious when they discovered that Paul, encouraged by John Eastman, had been secretly buying up more shares in Northern Songs, behind their backs. But, as Paul commented, no matter how harsh he was being portrayed, all he wanted was to be released by the others so that he could live his own life. "I think the other three are the most honest, sincere men I have ever met," he said in an interview. "I love them, I really do... But for my own sanity we must change the business arrangements we have. Only by being completely free of each other financially will we ever have any chance of coming back together as friends..."

The court case was set to begin on 19 February 1971 and, to make a point that he was fine, his debut single as a solo performer, 'Another Day', was released on the same date. It achieved Top 5 positions in both the UK and USA, but critics once again – despite it now being recognised

Right: Paul and Linda McCartney outside the Royal Courts of Justice in London for the first day of their hearing to dissolve the Beatles' partnership. 19th February 1971

as an excellent song, backed by the equally impressive 'Oh Woman Oh Why' – regarded it as little more than "just another song". Whatever the supposedly villainous McCartney produced in those early days was likely, it seemed, to be regarded as an easy target for media snipers.

Paul and Linda attended the opening day of his court case at the Royal Courts of Justice, him wearing the same dark suit he'd worn on the front cover of *Abbey Road*, looking happy and very confident. Written affidavits from his former bandmates read aloud in court by their lawyers weren't easy listening for him, but could've been a lot worse. Lennon's complaints were more against the Eastmans than Paul, although he did conclude that Paul was acting "selfishly and unreasonably"; George described him as often displaying a "superior attitude" but was happy to state that the by now world famous disagreement at Twickenham Film Studios portrayed in the film *Let it Be* had actually helped them to resolve their differences, but he still couldn't "understand why Paul acted as he did" in wanting to dissolve the partnership. Ringo, who never finds it easy to be rude about anybody,

described Paul as "the greatest bass player in the world" but also a very "determined" man who likes to "get his own way". Nothing very revealing or earth-shattering there, but Ringo was also shocked to have received the writ bringing the Beatles to an end.

Relieved that they could now return to America to finish their album together, and leave their lawyers to get on with the legal arguments, Paul and Linda flew to Los Angeles, working with the producer Jim Guercio. Determined to ensure this would be better than *McCartney*, Paul continually tinkered with the songs and fretted over the running order, so much so that a frustrated Guercio eventually departed feeling he was surplus to requirements.

Above: Allen Klein, outside London's Royal Courts of Justice, 19th February 1971.

Right: The McCartneys at Heathrow Airport, March 71

Chapter 2. 1970-71: The New Beginning 35

Good news arrived from London on 12 March that Paul had won the first stage of the court case – that Allen Klein should not have been appointed as their manager without Paul's consent. As happy as spring lambs they headed back to High Park Farm (to which they had added another 400 acres and 200 Highland sheep) for a few weeks' peace and calm. It was there that the title for the new album had been conceived. Driving through the Scottish countryside Paul had spotted a flock of sheep including some robust-looking males. "Ram," he said, would be the perfect title: "...strong and male... and succinct. Then there was the idea of ramming... pushing ahead strongly."

That was the way Paul intended to live his life from now on. *Ram* was released on 17 May 1971 and, although once again not very well-reviewed by the media, made it to No. 1 in the UK, and just one place behind in the USA. The album's fluorescent cover certainly portrayed Paul as a man not prepared to take too much nonsense from his former bandmates, if that was the way they wanted to play things out. Gripping a sheep between his legs with a pair of shears in his hand, he was ready to rumble. There were various little clues to illustrate that point on the inside cover: a photograph of two beetles screwing each other – not a difficult one to work out (although Paul denies that had even crossed his mind). And some of the lyrics in 'Oh Woman Oh Why' (the B-side on the first single) and 'Too Many People' (B-side on the second single released in the USA, 'Uncle Albert/Admiral Halsey'), were interpreted as Paul taking potshots at John and Yoko for some of their more unusual activities.

Paul would claim in later years that there was nothing too serious in any of the petulant remarks or images produced by either side; John also protested that lyrics from the song 'How Do You Sleep' from his album *Imagine* released that year was also just good clean fun, not a vicious attack at all: *The only thing you done was yesterday / And since you've gone you're just another day... / A pretty face may last a year or two / But pretty soon we'll see what you can do / The sound you make is muzac to my ears / You must've learned something in all of those years / Oh how do you sleep? / How do you sleep at night?*

Words can never hurt you... but bricks can. Rumour (or myth) has it that, on 12 March 1971, on the day that the Judge at the High Court in London ruled in Paul's favour, a car pulled up at Cavendish Avenue occupied by three well known musicians, one of whom jumped out, climbed over the wall and threw a brick through Paul's window. Imagine that.

Right: Portrait of Paul McCartney to publicise the outset of his solo career in 1970

Below: Promotional poster for 'Ram'

Chapter 3:
1971-72: Ram On

In April 1971 Allen Klein and the three other Beatles decided that they weren't going to appeal against the High Court's judgement against them and that Paul McCartney would be released from the partnership – all, but everything, he wanted. Or was it?

Freedom is a wonderful thing but it wasn't long before Paul started to think how great it would be to form another band and have another go. Not only that, lying in bed one night with ideas ricocheting around his head, he turned to Linda and said, "I'm going to form a band. Do you want to be in it?" Amazingly, given that she could barely play the piano at all, Linda said she'd be happy to give it a go. "She and I knew she was a novice while I was a veteran... but I liked the tone of her voice... I'd never sung with a woman before. All my harmonies to that date had been with males." Paul and Linda had only been married just over a year and hadn't spent one night apart, nor wanted to. On top of that, Linda was pregnant with their third child (Paul had adopted Heather when she was six). Unless they travelled together, played together, and took their children with them to... play together(!), it just wouldn't work. The stage was set. All they needed now was a band.

First to be contacted were the two session musicians that had contributed to the *Ram* sessions in New York through to the end – Denny Seiwell on drums and Hugh McCracken on guitar – along with their wives Monique and Holly. What they were expecting when invited to stay at Paul McCartney's property in the Scottish Highlands can only be guessed at, but it certainly wasn't High Park Farm. Despite being put up in a hotel in Campbeltown, neither of the two wives was impressed with the set-up; Holly McCracken wanted to return to America as soon as possible, as did Hugh with two little kids from a former marriage. Neither returned, but Seiwell promised that he and Monique would come back after visiting her family in France, as soon as Paul could find another guitar player.

Paul's next target was the former guitarist and vocalist with the Moody Blues, Denny Laine, who had sung lead vocals on their big hit back in 1964, 'Go Now' – one of Linda's favourite songs. Laine had previously known the Beatles quite well as Brian Epstein had also managed the Moody Blues for a brief period. For Denny it was just as well that Paul had made the call because he'd been struggling financially for some time and was basically living on a mattress at another former manager's office. Within a few hours Denny was heading up to High Park Farm.

An old outbuilding with a four-track recording machine from Abbey Road was set up as a studio – Rude Studio as Paul christened it – and work got underway almost immediately. By August they had put together eight rough tracks, which were then finished off at Abbey Road when they returned to London, primarily for Linda to give birth

Right: *Original Wings line-up. Clockwise from top: Laine, McCullough, Paul, Linda and Seiwell*

Chapter 3: 1971-72: Ram On 39

Chapter 3: 1971-72: Ram On

to their third daughter, Stella. It was a difficult birth and Paul found himself pacing up and down praying that both would be ok; they were, of course, thanks to a guardian angel he envisaged standing over them, spreading its golden wings. That's a good name...

The album was completed in record time and, following a lavish party in London's Leicester Square to introduce *Wild Life* and McCartney's new band, Wings, the album was released just before Christmas. As before, McCartney's third post-Beatles LP was torn to shreds by UK and US critics. It's not that bad at all, but had, once again, been rushed out unnecessarily. But that was Paul – softly softly catchee monkey would never be his catchphrase. Already he was planning to take to the road with his new live band, including his wife on keyboards even though she had only just started keyboard lessons with an elderly teacher across the road in Cavendish Avenue. It wasn't going well. To give the band a little more professional cover, Paul also employed guitarist Henry McCullough from the beautiful seaside town of Portstewart near Derry in Northern Ireland.

By February 1972 Wings had not only released their first single, 'Give Ireland Back to the Irish' – a protest song (which the BBC banned) condemning the shootings of 13 people by the British Army in Derry, on what became known as 'Bloody Sunday' – but had also organised (in the loosest terms imaginable) the band's first UK tour. In a hired van full of five musicians (!), Denny Seiwell's wife Monique, band equipment, two roadies (Ian Horne and Trevor Jones), three little girls, three dogs and a map, they headed off into the unknown. Nothing had been planned in any great detail; Paul's concept was to drive north and, wherever they landed, find the nearest University and offer to perform at an afternoon concert. Nottingham was the first, followed by shows in York, Hull, Newcastle, Lancaster, Leeds, Sheffield, Salford, Birmingham and Swansea. Despite several mistakes, chords being forgotten and songs being repeated due to a lack of material (four or five

of their own songs and a handful of rock 'n' roll classics, but no Beatles numbers), they went down a storm. What would you expect: 40p or 50p to watch Paul McCartney's new band play at your college in the afternoon? Brill!

The band seemed to enjoy it as well as they shared out handfuls of coins after each show, so much so that Paul (and possibly even Linda) now felt that a proper professional tour of Europe was on the cards. By July 1972, with two more UK Top 10 singles and plenty of time to write, rehearse and, at Abbey Road, start recording a bucketful of new material for their predicted double-album, *Red Rose Speedway*, Wings felt confident they were ready to take on Europe. The 'Wings Over Europe Tour' took in 28 shows across France, Belgium, Switzerland, the Netherlands, West Germany, Norway, Denmark, Sweden and Finland. Once again, however, there were no private jets, no limos, no tour bus... but there was a bus – a multi-coloured, open-top, double-decker full of deckchairs and mattresses and child playpens (yes, they joined in once again) and cuddly toys. Watching footage of the bus crawling along narrow roads at about 30mph with kids playing on the top deck looks pretty frightening, but they survived. When some stuffy critics argued that the McCartney children should be at nursery or school, Paul's response was, "Hey, it's a geography lesson." Everyone in Wings was chilled – perhaps too chilled.

This, it seemed, would be the first time Paul realised that European drug laws apply to ex-Beatles just the same as to everybody else. They had arranged for parcels of dope to be sent by post to hotels along the route and most of the time they got away with it. A package addressed to Denny Seiwell, however, had been posted to a hotel in Gothenburg, Sweden, but when they tried to collect it,

Left: Paul McCartney, 1972

Paul and Linda were arrested by local police. They were given a stiff warning not to do it again and had to pay a substantial fine, but much bigger drugs busts would be required in the future for either of them to consider such issues more seriously. When they returned to High Park Farm the local Scottish police were waiting to greet them following a tip-off they were growing dope in their greenhouse. Paul claimed the seeds had been a gift from a fan and they had assumed it would grow into something to eat. Another fine, £100, was paid and cheeky smirks caught on camera as they left the local magistrates' court.

Apart from a few drugs problems, all had been going pretty well for Wings so far. Work on *Red Rose Speedway* was progressing and two more Top 10 singles – the rather bizarre 'Mary Had a Little Lamb', which added a simple

Chapter 3: 1971-72: Ram On   43

tune to the well-known nursery rhyme Paul would recite to his daughters, and 'Hi Hi Hi', which in contrast was once again banned by the BBC due to its drug references.

The only rumblings of discontent among the band's hired musicians was that, at just £70 a week, they weren't being paid enough, and all had a good case to argue. It wasn't a terrible wage, but one might have expected slightly more from one of the world's most successful songwriters. The indication from Paul was that his money was currently tied up in Apple Corps while lawyers attempted to resolve the issues between McCartney, Klein and the other ex-Beatles. C'est la vie – that's the way it was (and remains) in the music business. Musicians deserve a decent wage. Everyone needs to live and let live. Or die. That would be one of the next items on Mr. McCartney's hit list.

On the converted double-decker bus for Wings' first European tour, Juan-les-Pins, France, 12th July 1972

Chapter 4:
1973-74 : Bond On The Run

1973 got off to a very good start with the release of a glorious new single from Wings, 'My Love', the first to be lifted from *Red Rose Speedway*, featuring Henry McCullough's inspired guitar solo. Yet another beautiful love song dedicated to Linda (who else?), 'My Love' made it to No. 9 in the UK and unexpectedly topped the charts in the USA. Within three months another single would be released to elevate the band to a much higher level of appreciation.

Red Rose Speedway hadn't got off to a good start in 1972 when the original producer Glyn Johns – well-known for his impressive canon of work with the likes of the Rolling Stones, Led Zeppelin, Bob Dylan and the Eagles – found the material he was listening to simply not good enough (or "shite", as he put it). Within four weeks he had walked out on the project and left Paul at the controls all by himself. With pressure from EMI, Paul eventually agreed to reduce the planned double album down to a single disc, meaning some decent songs (and one or two not so good) never made it onto the final track listing. There was one song recorded during these sessions, however, that certainly would have been good enough if it wasn't intended for somewhere else – on the soundtrack and as the title song for the next James Bond movie, *Live and Let Die*.

Paul, just like everybody else of a certain age, was a huge fan of the Bond films and had already expressed an interest in writing a Bond theme at some stage of his career. After the success of the Beatles spoof spy movie *Help!* in 1965, Paul had been approached to see if he'd be interested in writing a title song for the previous Bond film *Diamonds Are Forever*, but that had never progressed. For *Live and Let Die* one of the Bond producers, Albert R. Broccoli, contacted McCartney to see if he'd be interested – who wouldn't be? To write (and perform) a Bond theme was the key to a treasure chest. The usual Bond composer and arranger, the brilliant John Barry, wasn't available to take charge on this occasion as he was working on the London West End stage musical *Billy*, so Paul approached his old colleague George Martin (who had previously produced the theme songs for *From Russia with Love* and *Goldfinger*) to produce and orchestrate *Live and Let Die*.

Once agreed, Paul was sent a copy of the Ian Fleming novel, which he digested in one afternoon and then put together the title song the following day. Totally different to any of the previous seven Bond themes, it stood out just by nature of it being a rock song following a succession of brilliant vocalists: Matt Monro, Shirley Bassey, Tom Jones, Nancy Sinatra and Louis Armstrong. When George Martin delivered the song to Broccoli and his co-producer Harry Saltzman, rumour has it that they loved it but intended to offer the screen version to Thelma Houston or Aretha Franklin! As good as that would have been, George Martin had to dig in his heels and insist it was Paul McCartney and Wings or the deal was off. Not

Right: *Paul and Linda McCartney and Denny Seiwell attend the premiere of 'Live and Let Die' at the Odeon Leicester Square, London, 5th July 1973*

Chapter 4: 1973-74: Bond On The Run   45

only did they agree but also took it for granted that Martin would handle composing and arranging the film score as well, re-establishing him as one of rock music's pre-eminent producers. For Paul and co-writer Linda (who came up with the idea for the reggae section), and for Wings, this was a big leap forward for a band that, although reasonably successful, was still not being regarded too seriously by the public or media. After two drugs busts, two banned singles and two tours put together on a peppercorn budget, Wings needed something to promote them into pop music's higher echelons.

McCartney had agreed to put together a 55-minute TV extravaganza for Sir Lew Grade – now owner of the Beatles' music publishers, Northern Songs – as a way to placate him over the issue of some titles being credited to Paul and Linda McCartney, rather than just Paul, which deprived Grade of 50 per cent of the rights to new material since the Beatles had split. *James Paul McCartney* was aired by Grade's ATV in April 1973 in the US and a month later in the UK, made up of a series of old-fashioned musical pieces involving plenty of costumes and make-up and some comedy aspects. It wasn't brilliant, nor was it terrible, but it was an opportunity to launch the spectacular new single *Live and Let Die* and propel it into the UK and US Top 10s.

Wings set off on their first 'proper' UK tour to support *Red Rose Speedway* in May that year, supported by Brinsley Schwarz (featuring Nick Lowe). The tour took in 16 venues in England, Scotland and Wales, including three nights at London's Hammersmith Odeon. One show scheduled for 5 July at Stoke-on-Trent was cancelled to allow Wings and their partners to attend the world premiere for *Live and Let Die* at the Odeon Leicester Square, attended by Her Royal Highness Princess Anne. The film was a great success, as was George Martin's soundtrack LP, while the title song represented a significant turning point for both. 'Live and Let Die' was the first Bond theme ever to be nominated for an Oscar (it went to 'The Way We Were' from the film of the same name, sung by Barbra Streisand), and it also reopened the doors for McCartney and

Martin to work together once again on what would prove to be Wing's greatest achievement.

During Wings' 1973 UK tour Paul and Linda had taken advantage of a June break to spend time in southeast England looking for a new property that would provide an escape from the mayhem of London on a regular basis without having to travel all the way up to Scotland. What they found was a little place called Waterfall in Peasmarsh, East Sussex, near the beautiful town of Rye – one of the South East's seven historic Cinque Ports grouped together for defence against invasion back in the reign of Edward the Confessor (1042-66). They bought it for just over £42,000, initially as a weekend retreat but which would eventually become (and remains) Paul's primary residence.

So now he owned a very smart Regency townhouse in London (just up the road from Abbey Road Studios), a sprawling farm up in Scotland and a beautiful country estate in East Sussex... so of course, when it came to working on the next Wings album, Paul chose to record it at EMI Studios in... Lagos, Nigeria. Africa! Only Paul knows why – his sense of adventure, possibly – but he was pushing the barriers when it came to maintaining any loyalty among his band members who were already on the edge. Rehearsing up in Scotland before heading over to Lagos, Henry McCullough decided he'd had enough with the constant low wages and high level of interference from Paul as to how to play his guitar parts. On 14 July he packed his bags at the end of the day and drove home to London, never to return.

By this stage Denny Laine had paired up with an American model called Joanne (Jo Jo) La Patrie who had joined them on the European tour by bribing one of the roadies, one way or another. Paul, apparently, was the one she had her eyes on, but Denny became an acceptable substitute. Preparing to travel back down south for their flight to Lagos, Jo Jo, who was now

Right: *Paul McCartney, 1973*

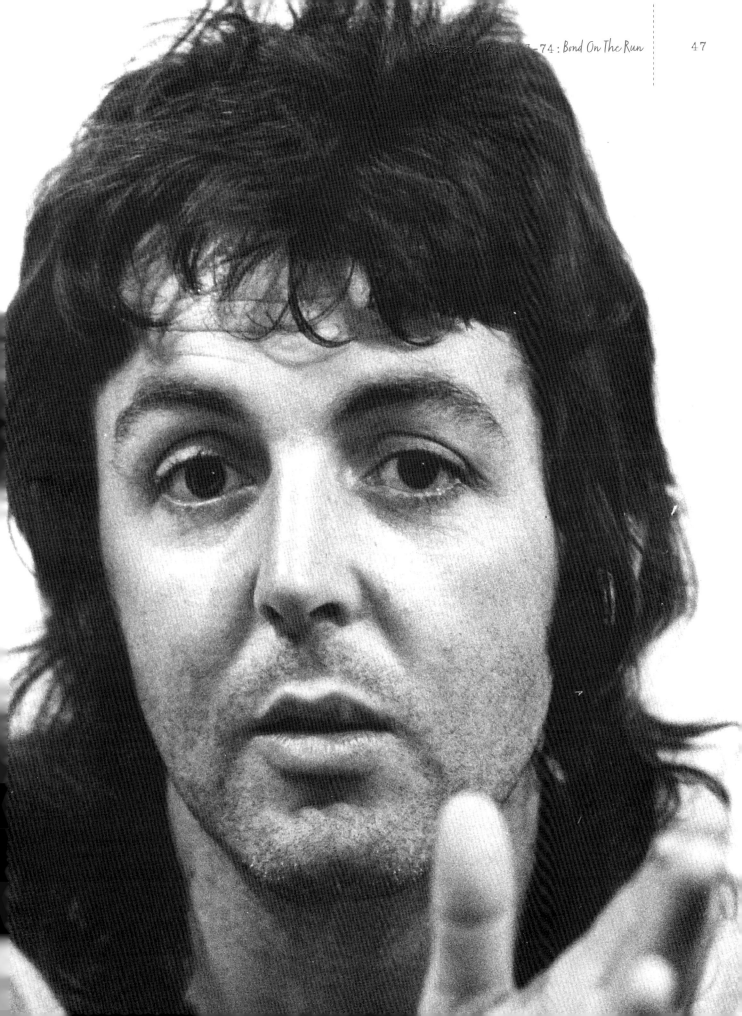

Another Day Paul McCartney
Life Beyond the Beatles

pregnant, went into labour and gave birth to their first child. Wonderful, but it wasn't going to make things any easier for Wings' trip to Africa. For the other Denny, drummer Seiwell, it all proved too much; the day before they were due to fly to Nigeria, he called Paul and quit. One can understand why. If he'd actually made it to Lagos he almost certainly would've wished he had. Paul, absolutely livid, took the other view: "Screw you. I will make an album you will wish you were on."

When the band - just the three of them now (plus Beatles sound engineer Geoff Emerick, two roadies and, of course, three kids) - arrived at EMI Lagos they discovered the studio was little more than a ramshackle hut full of dodgy equipment. Now add a hostile reception from local musicians when they arrived, regular monsoon storms, power cuts, Paul collapsing and being hospitalised with chest pains, an outbreak of cholera and, as if that wasn't enough, getting mugged at knifepoint by local thugs who stole their money, cameras, demo tapes and a notepad full of lyrics... Locals told them they were lucky to have survived at all. This was sounding more like the next James Bond movie - welcome to Lagos, Mr. McCartney!

Out of misery, as always, comes some of the greatest work of all time; the album that resulted, *Band on the Run*, is definitely up there. For seven weeks they tolerated probably some of the worst conditions for creating music since Paul's time back in Hamburg with the Beatles, but returned to London with the basic tracks of the greatest album Wings would ever make. Released in December 1973, the album was something of a slow burner and took 33 weeks on the UK charts before it made it to No. 1, where it remained for seven weeks. It also made it to No. 1 in the US charts three times in 1974 and went on to sell more than 6 million copies (now nearer 10m) worldwide. It was second and third in the UK/US annual charts and also became EMI's most successful album of the Seventies.

L to R: Denny Laine, Linda McCartney, Denny Seiwell, Henry McCullough and Paul McCartney performing on national TV, 1973

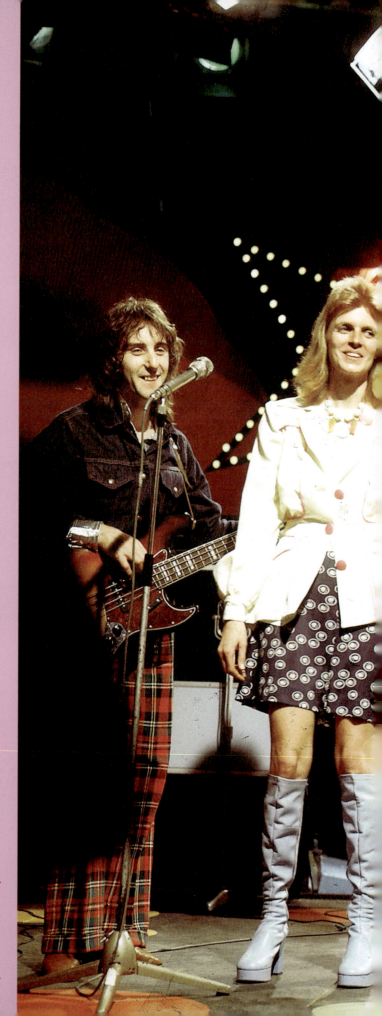

Chapter 4: 1973-74: Bond On The Run

Paul, Linda and Denny Laine putting the final touches to 'Band on the Run' at London's AIR Studios, 1973

At a time when there were increasing rumours that the Beatles might get back together again, it was the perfect ammunition Paul needed to be able to respond with "I don't need you anymore." His arsenal of verbal hand grenades was further strengthened when Allen Klein's contract as the Beatles' manager was not renewed at the end of 1973; John, George and Ringo had come to the conclusion that he wasn't a very nice, or honest, man. "If only we'd... Bang!" Paul would toss in his response: "I told you so." There were no apologies from the other Beatles as such, although John did make a comment that "possibly Paul's suspicions were right", and George Harrison backed that up with something along the lines of "thanks for getting us out of that". As Paul put it, he got the company back for them as well, not just for himself. He believes that if he had signed Klein's contract and not sued the other Beatles, they would have all ended up with nothing. In the end it took another six years before Klein was finally disassociated from the Beatles' finances and was paid $4.2m by Apple Corps. Not a bad result for a man who eventually, in 1979, went to prison for undeclared income during his time with Apple... for two months.

Paul and Ringo had always remained fairly close (Paul and Linda had written and performed on one song on Ringo's Top 10 album *Ringo*) and it did seem that some doors had been reopened for Paul to rekindle his friendship with John, now living permanently in New York. Even John had to admit that *Band on the Run* was a great album. In early 1974 Paul's US visa had been restored after having been suspended due to his drug charges in Sweden and Scotland, allowing several visits to see John and Yoko over the next few years. They would never be best mates again, but at least they were friendly to each other most of the time. George Harrison, however, didn't seem to want anything to do with Paul anymore.

McCartney's focus now was to concentrate on Wings and put together another new band, one that hopefully wouldn't see band members jumping ship at the last minute.

Paul McCartney rehearsing with Wings before their 12-city UK concert tour in 1973

Chapter 5:
1975-76: Wings Over The World

Paul did seem to prefer employing musicians with 'McC' in their name but this time he went so far as to employ a guitarist with the same name as the previous one, McCullough, but with the Scottish spelling – Jimmy McCulloch – who had previously played with the great Glasgow band Stone the Crows. McCulloch had already played on an album Paul produced for his brother Mike, entitled *McGear*, and been very impressed by Jimmy's guitar talents. He offered him a place in Wings almost immediately, despite being warned that there were some "Jekyll and Hyde" aspects to Jimmy's character where drugs and drinks were concerned...

Plenty of drummers were auditioned before finding a suitable replacement in Londoner Geoff Britton – a 31-year-old, hard-rocking but clean-living sort of guy who happened to have a black belt in karate. Hmmm. Moody, heavy drinking, drug-using McCulloch from Scotland versus England's equivalent to Kwai Chang Caine in the popular Seventies TV show *Kung Fu*. What could go wrong? The new line-up headed over to Nashville for six-weeks of rehearsals but it was apparent all too soon that Britton was not the most suitable choice to get on with the rest of the band – certainly not McCulloch who was being supplied with heavy drugs on a regular basis.

There were some positives – everyone enjoyed the laid-back Nashville vibe and it was there that Paul celebrated his 32nd birthday. From Linda he received an incredible gift in the shape of the double bass that had belonged to Elvis Presley's bass player, Bill Black; it was the instrument on which he had recorded the bass lines of 'Heartbreak Hotel'. Much better than a pair of socks. At SoundShop Studios in Nashville the new Wings also recorded their first single together, 'Junior's Farm' backed with the beautiful country and western number 'Sally G.' – such a cool, laid back song from a band that certainly wasn't. Arguments began to break out increasingly during rehearsals – McCulloch not impressed with Linda's keyboards, Paul not happy with some of Britton's drumming patterns on quieter numbers, Britton storming out of rehearsals on more than one occasion, McCulloch getting pulled over for dangerous driving while drunk, and none of them, including Denny Laine, being happy with the financial situation, despite promises of new contracts and wage increases.

At least financially the Beatles' partnership was finally dissolved on 19 December 1974 when the band were due to meet at the Plaza Hotel in New York to sign new contracts that would at last release millions of royalties. Unfortunately John (who only lived across the other side of Central Park) didn't turn up as he and Yoko's astrologer had advised them that the planets weren't quite in the right orbits, or something along those lines. Be a good name for an album though. *Venus and Mars*.

The Beatles' partnership was finally dissolved in January 1975 in London's High Court and Paul's other fragmented band

Right: Paul and Linda McCartney pose for a portrait celebrating the release of the album 'Band On The Run', December, 1973, Los Angeles, California

Chapter 5: 1975-76: Wings Over The World   55

Above: Wings together at London's Abbey Road Studios in November 1974 to record 'Venus And Mars'. Left to right: drummer Geoff Britton, Paul, Linda, Denny Laine and guitarist Jimmy McCulloch

headed over to New Orleans to record their next album at Sea-Saint recording Studio. Three songs-in, unfortunately, the other band members all decided they'd had enough of Geoff Britton's character and behavior. One morning he was paid off, told to pack his bags and frog-marched out of the building to be replaced by a much cooler and (they hoped) calmer New York session player, Joe English.

To finish off the album the band headed over to Wally Heider Studios in Los Angeles and, despite getting pulled over for jumping a light and Linda being charged for possession of marijuana, everything went reasonably well. On 1 March 1975 Paul and Linda collected two Grammy awards for *Band on the Run*, with John, Yoko and David Bowie in the audience, followed by a wrap party for *Venus and Mars* on the Queen Mary cruise liner docked at Long Beach. The guest list was a veritable who's who of music and movie stars, most notably George Harrison, with whom Paul was able to have a friendly conversation for the first time in years. It was also there that Paul met Michael Jackson for the first time and they were able to chat and discuss the possibility of working together in the near future. It was also the first time the McCartneys insisted on

Chapter 5: 1975-76: *Wings Over The World* 57

a meat-free party menu – they had become vegetarians earlier that year.

Venus and Mars was released at the end of May 1975 and went straight to No. 1 in both the UK and USA. Having achieved such a level of success over the last few months, and despite the various issues within the band, Paul was convinced this was the right time for Wings to move up another gear and prepare for a gigantic world tour. The band's rehearsals got underway at Elstree Studios north of London and went on for the next four months in preparation for the 'Wings Over the World Tour', setting off in Southampton on 9 September 1975 and taking in the UK, Australia, Europe, North America and Japan. Thanks to the Japanese authorities getting wind of Paul's 1973 drugs bust in Scotland, however, they refused to allow them in and the shows had to be cancelled. Overall, the tour went very well, especially Paul's acceptance of the need to include a few Beatles songs – 'Lady Madonna', 'The Long and Winding Road', 'I've Just Seen a Face', and two solo acoustic numbers – 'Blackbird' and 'Yesterday'. As anticipated, they brought the house down.

During a Christmas break in the tour Paul and Linda paid an unexpected visit to see John and Yoko and reportedly got on very well, like old friends. Once again big organisations were putting together ridiculously generous offers for the Beatles to get together again, with numbers in the region of $50m being waved in

Below: Promotional poster for 'Venus and Mars'

Venus and Mars are alright tonight.

front of their faces for putting together a one-off show. Even today that sounds ridiculous. How seriously it was taken is not really known but something that did annoy at least Paul was EMI's decision to cash-in on this newfound Beatlemania by releasing all 22 of the UK's Beatles singles, on the same day, plus, for the first time, 'Yesterday' coupled with 'I Should Have Known Better'. Paul felt this could have a negative impact on Wings' singles and possibly even their album sales, but he needn't have worried. When the single 'Silly Love Songs' was released from their next album, *Wings at the Speed of Sound* in 1976, it made it to Nos. 2/1 in the UK and US charts – going on to become one of the band's most successful singles ever. It was time to celebrate.

Celebrations, however, were very much muted when Paul received the news that his father Jim, suffering from severe arthritis and the effects of life as a heavy smoker, had passed away. It was two days before Wings were due to restart their 'Wings Over the World Tour' in Copenhagen and Paul, being the showman he is, decided to carry on as if nothing had happened. Not even the band knew. Paul had visited his father at his home earlier in March and was well aware that Jim had not long to go. The funeral was held on 22 March and the band were due to play in Berlin the following day. Using private planes it's feasible Paul could have made it to Birkenhead for the service and returned in time for the show, but chose not to. As his brother Mike put it: Paul "would never face that kind of thing".

Paul McCartney on stage, Berlin, 1976

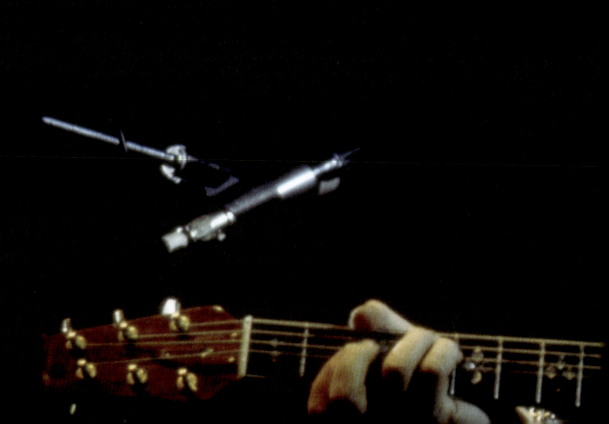

Chapter 5: 1975-76: Wings Over The World   59

Chapter 6:
1976-79: Wings Over New Waves

The second leg of the 'Wings Over the World Tour' was intended to set out across the USA in April to support both *Venus and Mars* and *Wings At the Speed of Sound*; released just 10 months later, it had also made it to No. 1 in America and to No. 2 in the UK. Unfortunately the start of the USA tour had to be delayed for nearly a month when Jimmy McCulloch broke his finger – officially explained as an accident when he slipped getting out of the bath at the Hotel George V in Paris. That much was true – Wings were in the hotel – the actual cause was a drunken punch-up with the American pop star David Cassidy after McCulloch had called him a "fag" and swung a punch; Cassidy had defended himself and put McCulloch down on the canvas.

Eventually the tour restarted on 3 May 1976 at Tarrant County Convention Centre in Fort Worth, Texas – Paul's first show in the USA since 29 August 1966 – a big moment for him and everybody else who attended. When he walked onto the stage alone he was given a 15-minute standing ovation before so much as a note had been played. Americans loved the Beatles, and Paul McCartney just as much. The US leg traversed across America for almost two months through to 23 June 1976, with many of the concerts professionally recorded and cherry-picked for release as the triple album *Wings over America* in December that year.

Once again the McCartney children were all in tow along with their housekeeper/nanny Rose Martin and a tutor for Heather, now 13. To make things more bearable, up to a point, a private jet was laid on after every show to take the band to the nearest of one of four rented homes in New York, Chicago, Dallas and Los Angeles. Equipment and an army of crew and technicians travelled by road in three enormous trucks in convoy, each with one of the words in sequence on their roofs: 'WINGS', 'OVER', 'AMERICA'.

From a man who'd desired simple college gigs crossing the UK in an old van, things had moved on unrecognisably in the last six years. From hordes of spotty students at 50p a ticket, Wings were now attracting ex-Beatles (George and Ringo in Toronto), ex-wives of Presidents (Jackie Kennedy turned up unannounced at Madison Square Garden in New York and wanted to hangout with the guys in their changing room), and an endless supply of music and movie stars (Cher, Dustin Hoffman, Diana Ross, Elton John, Jack Nicholson etc etc). Among the 'common people' such scenes began to draw comparisons with Beatlemania back in the Sixties. Paul was back and Wings were up there on clouds among the Rock Gods. The 'Wings Over America' section of the tour alone had turned over more than £3 million from which McCartney had paid himself over £95K. Compared to his 10 years with the Beatles, Paul was happy to reveal: "I have earned more money than I have ever earned in all the so-called boom years put together."

Much of the profit was used to expand Paul's own production company created back in 1970 when starting out as a solo artist. Initially known as McCartney Productions, it was basically run from his accountant's

Right: Paul McCartney backstage at Ahoy in Rotterdam, Netherlands on March 25th 1976

Chapter 6: 1976-79: *Wings Over New Waves*   61

office and would allow him to control his own work without interference from others. From 1976 the company would go on to be known as McCartney Productions Limited and finally MPL Communications. Their first offices were rented in Soho's Greek Street before buying their own property just up the road, a lovely five-story Edwardian building at 1 Soho Square, 100 yards or so from Ronnie Scott's world-famous jazz club and two doors away from the British Board of Film Censors (or Classification since 1984). Other funds went on extending ownership of land around their properties in Scotland and Peasmarsh,

in an effort to provide more security and privacy from obsessive fans that would turn up from time to time and expect to be invited in for tea and cakes.

Financially, as always, there were still major issues within the band, particularly when it came to wages. When Denny Laine threatened to quit Wings it's been reported that he was given a £30K bonus and his wages rose from £70 a week to around £70K a year. That was a bit more like it. At the end of the world tour all of the musicians were given a $10K bonus, but none had been happy with their

Jimmy McCulloch, Denny Laine, Linda and Paul, 1976

Chapter 6: 1976–79: *Wings Over New Waves*

weekly salaries. It appeared that both Jimmy McCulloch and Joe English were spending considerable amounts of their income on drugs, which couldn't have helped Jimmy's problems with mood swings. It had reached a point where, at the end of a gig in Boston one night, he refused to return to the stage for an encore. McCartney physically dragged him back with the promise of a good kicking if he didn't get out there.

Here were the two extremes of the rock business, or just about any other business come to that. Wealthy bosses and hard-up, unhappy workers. Everyone needed a rest after a year-long world tour and that decision had already been made when the news arrived that Linda was pregnant with their fourth child: first son James would arrive on 12 September 1977 at almost exactly the same time as music's own red-faced, spitting, screaming offspring – punk rock.

Like most rock dinosaurs, Paul wasn't overly impressed when it arrived on the scene, but he did have a nearly 15-year-old daughter called Heather, so there was little chance of ignoring it. And he had to admit that there was something very exciting about many of these young, new wave artists. Keeping things simple and down to earth might be the way to go for Wings as well... Sod it. Let's go and record the next album on a yacht off the coast of the US Virgin Islands.

It was actually Denny Laine's idea – a lover of boats and sailing who had recently visited Rod Stewart while recording on the Record Plant's floating studio off the coast of Los Angeles. Surprisingly (or maybe not so surprisingly?) Paul went along with it and the adventure got underway on 30 April 1977 with the recording studio set up on a 100ft long yacht called *Fair Carol*, plus a trimaran for the McCartneys to live on, and an old wartime minesweeper for the band and crew. It wasn't quite the relaxed idyll they'd been hoping for thanks to a few slip injuries, cases of sunburn, complaints about the noise and concerns about the use of dope on board. After a month or so at sea (just), the band returned to the UK with the basic tracks for their sixth studio album, *London Town*.

Throughout the summer that year the McCartneys and their band headed up to Scotland for more rehearsals and songwriting, with one sunny afternoon producing a particular number that would go on to be the UK's best-

Wings perform 'Mull of Kintyre' with the Campbeltown Pipe Band on comedian Mike Yarwood's Christmas Special, BBC Television Centre, London on 10th December 1977.

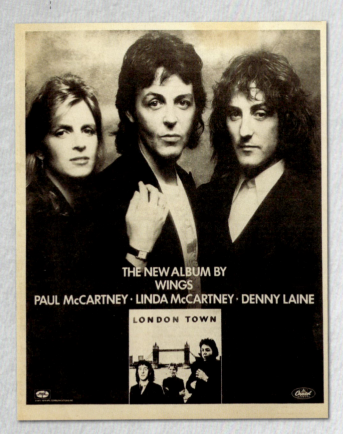

selling single of all time – 'Mull of Kintyre'. Co-written with Denny Laine, his presence helps to explain why it was probably the best Wings song lyrically and up there with some of McCartney's best work with the Beatles, at least poetically. Released in November 1977 with 'Girl School' as a double A-side, it made it to No. 1 in the UK within three weeks and stayed there for nine more. When it comes to best-selling singles in the UK, it's still in fourth place having sold well over 4 million copies.

One thing apparent, however, if you check to see who played on 'Mull of Kintyre', is that Jimmy McCulloch and Joe English didn't – once again Wings were down to just three members. McCulloch's behaviour had become so unacceptable at times (throwing Linda's chickens' fresh eggs against the wall in a fit of boredom and rage, for example) that Paul kicked him off the farm; and Joe's drug problem was becoming such an issue both mentally and physically that he returned to the USA for treatment.

Chapter 6: 1976-79: *Wings Over New Waves*

Happily, Joe cleaned himself up, found religion and formed his own Christian band with which he still performs to this day. Jimmy went on to play with various other bands including the Small Faces but, within two years, tragically died as a result of a drug overdose.

London Town was released in March 1978 to reasonable success and McCartney faced up once again to the inconvenience of having to find another new guitarist and drummer. They recruited two Londoners – Laurence Juber on guitar and Steve Holley on drums – both very talented session players who gave their all at rehearsals and during recording of what would become Wings' final album, *Back to the Egg*. His Capitol contract having come to an end in the USA, this was McCartney's first release on Columbia Records, making him the highest paid recording artist in the world. Released in June 1979 as a reflection of his efforts to embrace new wave and simplify everything back to their basics, (just as he'd tried to achieve with the Beatles 10 years earlier), the result was an album that's not bad but the least well-received of Wings' output. What came through from its vinyl grooves more than anything else was tiredness. McCartney had had enough of being in a band once again. "My enthusiasm had peaked," he said. Just like 1969, he was thinking about going solo for the second time.

Top Left: Press advert for 'London Town'

Left: Paul and Linda McCartney with the Rolling Stones' Ronnie Wood, backstage at the Palladium in New York City on June 19, 1978

Above: And backstage with Mick Jagger (left) and Bill Wyman (centre) at The Palladium, New York City.

Chapter 7:
1979-86: *War And Peace*

In 1979 Paul and Linda bought a 150-acre ranch near the Tanque Verde River in the foothills of the Rincon Mountains, northeast of Tucson, Arizona. Linda loved Arizona as much as anywhere in the world; it was where she had married her first husband Mel See in 1962 and where their daughter Heather was born. And there, more than anything else, she loved riding her horse: "I feel like I'm in heaven," she said, "heaven on earth... I just love it."

Coincidentally it was on 27 March 1979 that Eric Clapton married George Harrison's ex-wife Pattie Boyd in Tucson, because, he claimed, "the weather is so nice". In actual fact Eric was there because the next day he was performing in Tucson in a concert with the blues legend Muddy Waters. Not many friends and family attended the actual wedding so, in May, they held a celebratory wedding party at their home in Surrey, England. This time the 200-strong guest list created a virtual rock 'n' roll living museum, with many stars getting up on stage to take part in a giant jam that evening, including George Harrison, Ringo Starr and Paul McCartney playing together for the first time in 10 years. John Lennon hadn't been invited to the party but called Eric to wish him well and made the point that, if he'd known about the event, he would have come along, too. Who knows what that might have resulted in...

However, playing alone once again was dominating Paul's mind at the time and, from June to August 1979, he worked on his second genuine solo album. Performing everything himself with recordings taking place at his home studios in Peasmarsh and Scotland, *McCartney II* was another typical example of Paul being bold enough to dive in at the deep end with few concerns as to what people might think. It sold well, making Nos. 1 and 3 in the UK and US but, with much of it featuring Paul's new arsenal of electric synth equipment, a lot of people didn't like much of it at all.

With a second solo album out of his bloodstream Paul now needed to turn his attention to various other projects to bring 1979 to an end and welcome in the Eighties. No one could have imagined how awful the next 12 months would prove for everybody.

Wings had undertaken a 19-date UK tour from November through to Christmas, with four nights at the Royal Court Theatre in Liverpool, 10 nights at various locations in London and two at the Apollo in Glasgow being the highlights, particularly their performance of 'Mull of Kintyre' in Scotland when the Campbeltown Pipe Band unexpectedly marched on stage, causing such fan frenzy that the roof was almost blown off.

The tour came to an end with the final night of four Concerts for the People of Kampuchea at London's

Right: *Wings with Laurence Juber (far left) and Steve Holley (2nd right) aboard the Royal Irish Ferry on the River Mersey In Liverpool, 1979*

Chapter 7: 1980-86: *War And Peace*   69

Chapter 7: 1980-86: *War And Peace*   71

Hammersmith Odeon to raise money for war-torn Cambodia. Organised by McCartney and Austrian politician Kurt Waldheim, Wings performed on 29 December along with Paul's Rockestra, a supergroup (which had performed on *Back to the Egg*) including members of the Who, Pink Floyd and Led Zeppelin.

From 1978 Peasmarsh had become the McCartneys' regular home and, in 1979, Paul had purchased the adjacent Lower Gate Farm (reinstating its original name of Blossom Wood Farm) with its 160 acres of land and various outbuildings including stabling for horses. It was where the family would be at their happiest, with a brand new house (designed by Paul) eventually completed in 1981. That year he also bought more land and property in nearby Icklesham, about a 20-minute drive from Peasmarsh. It included an old windmill that had been standing there since 1790, known as Hogg Hill Mill. The mill and adjacent buildings would eventually be converted into his main recording location, known as Hog Hill Mill Studio, completed in 1985. (Why the second 'g' was removed from the original name is a good question.)

In the New Year the McCartneys set off for a planned 11-date tour of Japan that had been postponed back in 1975 because of the drug charges in Sweden and Scotland. The family, band and crew arrived at Tokyo's Narita International Airport on 16 January 1980 on two flights from London and Los Angeles, all slightly nervous of the reception that might await them from Japanese customs, given their previous history. Most of the band and crew sailed through, but when the McCartneys' flight from LA arrived about 30 minutes later, a disaster was about to unfurl. As Paul strolled slowly and casually through customs and immigration he is pulled over for a luggage inspection; within minutes the customs officer rifling through Paul's shirts and underwear

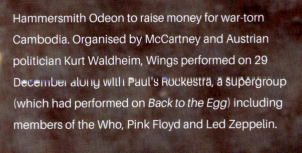

Paul and Linda McCartney, 1980. Was he framed...?

McCartney jailed in Japan

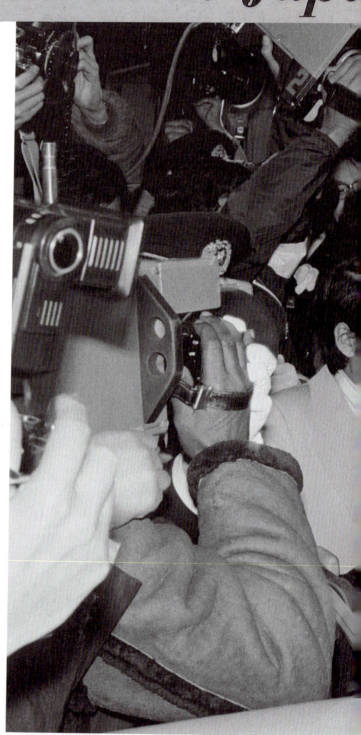

finds a clear plastic bag and peers at it incredulously. This could not be happening. The bag holds half a pound of marijuana. There follows a long period of every bag and instrument case being torn apart by customs officers until, eventually, Linda, the children and Laurence Juber (who had travelled with them) are allowed to leave. Paul is arrested, charged and taken to jail.

Paul was to spend 10 days incarcerated, facing up to the reality that he might be given a lengthy prison sentence. Obviously the tour was cancelled and the crew and equipment returned to the UK; musicians, who had all been issued with first class round-the-world tickets, were allowed to head off anywhere they wanted to, free of charge. But all were hugely disappointed in terms of how much income they were losing overall – all, for once, had been put on generous wages for the tour and possibly beyond with a promise of another American tour already in the pipeline.

How, or why it happened, remains something of a mystery. Some speculation at the time suggested Yoko tipped off the Japanese police that Paul would be carrying dope, which is ridiculous. Others suggested Paul may have done this deliberately. That sounds even more ridiculous and was totally unbelievable at the time, but now, more than 40 years later, it seems feasible given that Paul doesn't seem to deny such claims too adamantly. Maybe, it seems,

Right: Paul McCartney leaves a Tokyo Detention Center following release after 10 days in prison for attempting to smuggle marijuana into Japan

Chapter 7: 1980-86: War And Peace   73

JOHN LENNON SHOT DEAD

he'd just had enough and wanted Wings to come to an end dramatically with free publicity across the world. That may, he admitted many years later, have been his motivation. "It was as if I wanted to get caught," he said. The band felt completely under-rehearsed and he "got myself busted to get out of it". Just like back in 1970 when he was desperate to escape the Beatles, Paul was obviously not in a good place. But 10 years in a Japanese prison cell could have been a lot worse.

Instead, finally released with just a ticking off and a hefty fine, Paul returned to his house in East Sussex and did what most felons do once released from prison – lick their wounds and work on music for a Rupert the Bear animated film he'd been planning for years. It was probably the perfect cure for his miserable state of mind, bringing back happier memories from his childhood when life was much simpler. Certainly it was the end of Wings; as Laurence

Left: Paul McCartney, visibly shaken by the news of John Lennon's murder in New York, enters AIR Studios in London the following day

Juber put it, the Japanese incident had "sucked the momentum out of Wings". Or as McCartney put it, he'd always been looking forward to an opportunity to be able to say: "Wings folded."

Denny Laine was particularly angry about the financial implications of the tour being cancelled; once he'd discovered what was going on in Japan he departed almost immediately and jumped on a plane to a music conference in France to set up a record deal for his own solo album. Once signed, he headed back to London to concentrate on that. He was the only member of Wings who would hang around long enough to work on Paul's next solo album, *Tug of War*, but the other two returned to being session players. In June 1980 Wings held their final rehearsals at Finchden Manor in Tenterden, Kent, but nothing of any importance came from it. The band Wings was slowly fading away. It was sad, but what was to happen six months later overshadowed everything else.

On the morning of 9 December 1980, Paul received a call from MPL Communications to inform him that his closest ever friend, John Lennon, had been murdered. Stunned, and not knowing what to do with himself, Paul decided to travel to AIR Studios in London for a booked recording session where he could be with George Martin and be allowed to grieve together. Denny Laine was there, too, and they even managed to get some recording done, but Paul was clearly distraught throughout the day. In the afternoon he took a call from Yoko in New York and more tears were shed before Paul decided to head home. Outside the studio, unsurprisingly, were crowds of journalists wanting to know how Paul was feeling. His ultimate response, "It's a drag, isn't it?", while chewing gum, broadcast on every TV channel around the world that evening, would be something hanging around his neck for years to come. Why someone so desperately upset, but trying hard not to show it, should be punished so heartlessly for such an off-the-cuff remark sums up how cruel the British media could be in those times. Once back home,

behind drawn curtains, said Paul, "I wept like a baby."

Keeping himself in the shadows during a period of almost national mourning, Paul and Linda did fly over to New York to spend some time with Yoko before returning to the UK to continue working on *Tug of War*. On 1 February 1981 Paul, Linda and Denny Laine flew to George Martin's AIR Studios in Montserrat, where over the next few weeks they would be joined by a virtual cavalcade of world-famous musicians including Ringo Starr, Stevie Wonder, Carl Perkins, session drummer Steve Gadd and bass supremo Stanley Clarke; later, at AIR's London Studios, would arrive session drummer Dave Mattacks, Roxy Music's sax player Andy Mackay, and perhaps most importantly ex-10cc's guitarist and songwriter Eric Stewart, who would go on to collaborate with Paul very closely over the next five years.

With a long list of such stars on hand, Denny Laine began to feel rather surplus to requirements; once back in London, he just stopped turning up, at least making it unnecessary for Paul to fire him. Laine's announcement was that he had left Wings because Paul would no longer tour with the band, partly due to death threats he'd received since the murder of John Lennon. Laine was also very unhappy that his wife Jo Jo hadn't been allowed to accompany him on the trip to Montserrat, which he blamed to be a partial cause for their marriage breakdown. There was no way they would work together again. Wings really had come to a rather sad end. Said Paul: "The idea of working with Wings again would have just been limiting."

The proof was in the Tugging. *Tug of War*, without a great deal of input from Denny Laine, proved to be Paul McCartney's best album since *Wings at the Speed of Sound* and remains one of his best ever solo LPs. It made it to No. 1 on both sides of the Atlantic – his first album since *Venus and Mars* to achieve that – while the first single taken from it, 'Ebony and Ivory' with Stevie Wonder, went on to become McCartney's only double No. 1 hit in the UK/USA

since the Beatles. Furthermore the *Tug of War* sessions were so productive that several tracks were held over for McCartney's next album, *Pipes of Peace*, released two years later. It was nowhere near as good as *Tug of War* but his collaboration with Michael Jackson on two of the tracks added a new dimension to Paul's future in several ways.

Paying a visit down to Paul's new home at Blossom Wood Farm, 22-year-old Michael asked Paul if he could give him any career advice. Investing in song publishing was Paul's response, having already bought the publishing rights to a wide collection of popular music for MPL Communications including songs from the Buddy Holly and Carl Perkins back catalogues and various musicals including *Annie*, *La Cage aux Folles*, *Grease*, *High Society* and *Guys and Dolls*. But he didn't possess any Lennon/McCartney compositions – still owned by Sir Lew Grade's ATV Music. Taking on Paul's good advice, Jackson replied: "I'm going to buy your songs one day." In August 1985, using the huge amount of spare cash he made from the sales of his album *Thriller* (with Paul

RIGHT: Taken in 1984 during the filming of a video for 'So Bad', the B side of Paul's No. 1 single, 'Pipes of Peace'. Paul and Linda are joined by Ringo Starr and Eric Stewart

Above: Michael Jackson and Paul McCartney from the cover of their single 'The Girl is Mine'

Chapter 7: 1980-86: *War And Peace*

appearing on 'The Girl is Mine') Jackson went on to buy ATV Music, therefore owning Northern Songs and the Lennon/McCartney song catalogue, much to Paul's fury. He and Yoko had tried to buy the catalogue back in 1981 but to no avail. (In 2017, however, Paul managed to reacquire much of the Beatles material from Sony/ATV Music in a confidential settlement under the US Copyright Act of 1976 regarding material written before 1978.)

The combined impact of *Tug of War* and *Pipes of Peace* were as good as it would get for Paul McCartney through to almost the end of the decade. His work with George Martin on the Rupert the Bear animation project *Rupert and the Frog Song* would finally be released in 1983 with the single 'We All Stand Together' to considerable media mockery, but it was actually not bad and children loved it, so where's the harm? Later shown as a 13-minute short at the premiere of McCartney's

attempt at Hollywood superstardom, *Rupert* was certainly more enjoyable than that night's main feature, *Give My Regards to Broad Street*; released in 1984 it was, in a word, dire, although the accompanying soundtrack couldn't fail to be worth a listen considering it included several of Paul's greatest ever Beatles songs. As for 1986's album *Press to Play*, back on Capitol after disagreements with Columbia, perhaps the less said the better. It simply wasn't very good

What had proved a difficult decade was, in many ways, rescued by Paul's involvement, on 13 July 1985, as the headlining act at one of rock music's greatest ever moments – Live Aid, in support of Ethiopia's starving population. Paul had joined many other stars to perform on the single 'Do They Know it's Christmas' in 1984, which went on to surpass Paul's 'Mull of Kintyre' as the UK's best selling single. When it was decided to hold parallel one-day summer festivals the following year in London and Philadelphia, Bob Geldof had no hesitation in asking Paul to headline the event because, "Beatles music," he said, "evokes more emotional response than any other." George Harrison and Ringo were also invited to take part but both declined.

Opening at London's Wembley Stadium at 12 noon with Status Quo playing 'Rockin' All Over the World', the day's overall show stealer was probably Queen's stupendous performance of 'Bohemian Rhapsody', but when it came to the climax of what had been a very memorable and emotional day, there was no one better than Paul McCartney to bring it all to a fitting conclusion with 'Let it Be'. Despite huge technical PA problems resulting in several of the first few minutes of the song being inaudible, the audience took responsibility and started singing the words for him. When Paul's vocals finally made it through to the 75,000 crowd, and to a TV audience of almost 2 billion around the world, the response was stunning. When 'Let it Be' came to an end and McCartney stood on stage alongside

Right: Paul McCartney in the studio, 1984

Chapter 7: 1980-86: *War And Peace*   79

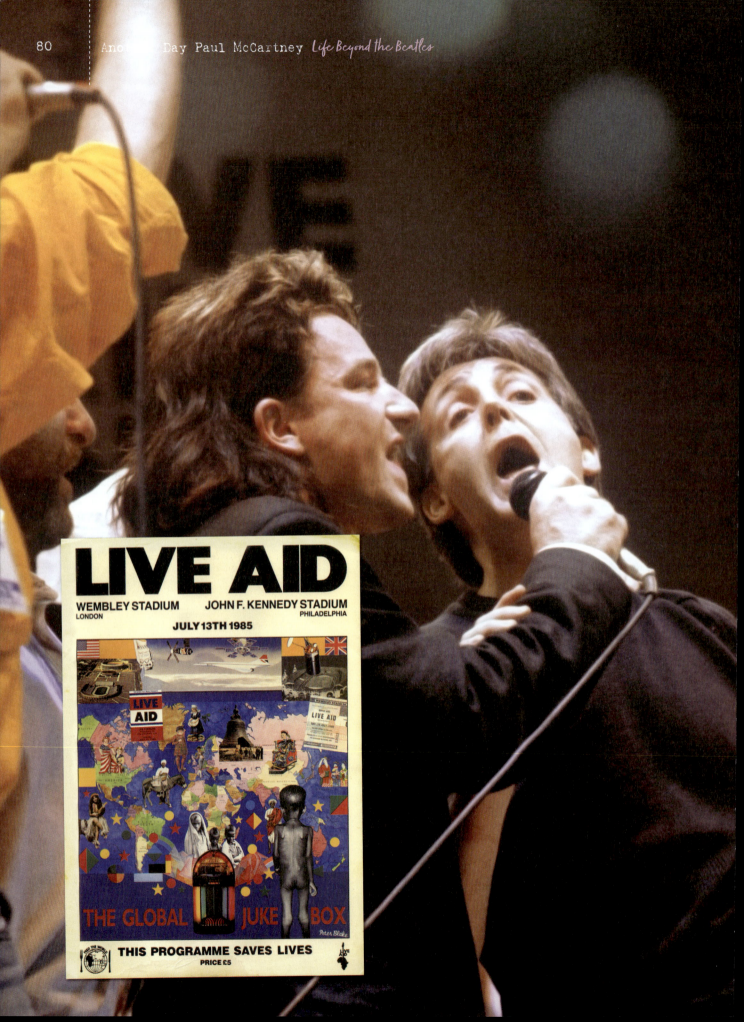

Geldof, raising Bob's arm aloft, it seemed as if both were being hailed as heroes for their contribution to such a worthy cause. Geldof certainly deserved such recognition, further still when Paul and Pete Townshend lifted him onto their shoulders.

For Paul, after a considerable lack of respect from the media and some elements of the public over the last few years, it was good just to welcome him back into the fold. In January 1988 there was further recognition when the Beatles were inducted into the Rock & Roll Hall of Fame – the first non-Americans to receive such an accolade in only the third ceremony of its kind ever to be held. It was well-deserved for all three remaining Beatles (and for the one who tragically couldn't be there) and all accepted the invitation. That is, until Paul discovered George, Ringo and Yoko were suing him over an issue regarding an extra one per cent of Beatles song catalogue sales being paid to him when he switched back to Capitol from Columbia in 1986. To everyone's disappointment, Paul boycotted the event. He would, he said, have felt a "complete hypocrite". After almost 20 years since the Beatles had split, some things, it seemed, would never change.

Live Aid, Wembley Stadium, London, 13 July 1985. L to R: Bono, Paul McCartney, Andrew Ridgeley, Freddie Mercury, Jody Watley and David Bowie

Left: Official Live Aid programme

Chapter 8:
1987-93: Animals, Elvis And Classical Gas

As the Nineties loomed it seemed Paul McCartney was determined to make some dramatic changes in his life in an effort to revive and improve his seemingly declining career. Since going solo in 1970 Paul had employed various business managers with limited success but, in 1987, at the recommendation of Linda's brother, John Eastman, 37-year-old Richard Ogden, the former head of Polydor Records, was employed as manager for both Paul and Linda. A three-year plan was put together to get Paul back into the charts with new albums, singles and, after almost 10 years, a world tour to support those record sales.

For Linda, Ogden would concentrate on her career as a photographer and on helping her produce merchandise to publicise her and Paul's conversion to vegetarianism since 1975 – something which had become increasingly important to both of them over the last few years. A short time later she would get involved with the Pretenders' Chrissie Hynde and the TV comedy writer Carla Lane, both passionate supporters of animal rights, with Blossom Wood Farm soon becoming a virtual sanctuary for any injured creatures that needed help. It was through Chrissie Hynde that Linda also met Peter Cox, chief executive of the Vegetarian Society, who would go on to help her create her own hugely successful business, Linda McCartney Foods, in 1991. That same year her first book, *Linda McCartney's Home Cooking*, was published by Bloomsbury and would go on to be their top-selling title for several years.

Things had certainly kicked off for Linda, but for Paul, even with Richard Ogden's assistance, he was still struggling to come up with something new and interesting to win back the many fans that had drifted away in recent years. In 1987 at Hog Hill Mill Studios, Paul had been jamming with a succession of old friends playing classic old rock 'n' roll numbers and decided to turn it into an album. Over two days 20 tracks were recorded live in the studio, of which 11 would go on to be included on the album *Choba B CCCP* ('Back Again in the USSR') released in 1988.

For Richard Ogden, that was far from being the sort of material he had envisaged as being necessary to revitalise Paul's career around the world; it was Ogden's idea to release the album initially only in the USSR, where it proved hugely popular among pop music-craving Russians. For a wider audience Ogden helped put together a new McCartney compilation, *All the Best!*, made up of solo material from 1970 onwards, but something new was needed with another, younger collaborator, who could create the sparks needed for a comeback album. After a great deal of thought it was decided to approach Elvis Costello, one of the biggest new wave stars from the Seventies, whose career and reputation over the last decade had rocketed. Says Ogden: "Paul felt it was helpful that they both had an Irish heritage and Liverpool family roots in common. But one of the things Paul liked best about Elvis's songwriting was his strength as a lyricist. Paul

Right: Paul and Linda McCartney, 1987

Chapter 8: 1987-92: Animals, Elvis And Classical Gas   83

'New World Tour', Orlando, Florida, 1993. L to R: Robbie McIntosh, Wix Wickens, Paul and Blair Cunningham

Chapter 8: 1987-92: Animals, Elvis And Classical Gas 85

sensed his own melodies and ideas could be excitingly compatible with Costello's literate style."

It sounded a perfect plan but, despite the two writers' mutual respect and Scouse roots, there were clearly considerable disagreements between them. The album eventually released was a great improvement on Paul's previous two LPs, with the four best songs probably those he and Costello had co-written, but it was not the album Costello expected. Once Elvis had left the building, Paul brought in alternative producers and re-recorded and remixed much of it.

Some positives from the sessions were that Paul, with Ogden's help, had put together probably his best solo line-up of tour musicians to date with guitarists Hamish Stuart (Average White Band) and Robbie McIntosh (the Pretenders), drummer Chris Whitten (who had been retained since working on the Russian album), and multi-instrumentalist Paul 'Wix' Wickens (who has gone on to become Paul's musical director for over 30 years). Linda would also join them on keyboards for what would be (and remains) McCartney's biggest foreign excursion ever – the 1989 to '90 'Paul McCartney World Tour' comprising 103 shows spread over 10 months across Europe, North America, UK, Brazil and, surprisingly given what had happened 10 years earlier, six nights in Tokyo, Japan. What the audiences around the world loved the most was that, for the first time, more than 50 per cent of each night's setlist would be made up of Beatles numbers. Sighs of relief around the world were audible.

Financially, despite the costs required for a crew of over 250, tons of equipment loaded into 17 huge trucks, security staff, vegetarian catering, merchandise sales etc, world touring had become something of a money tree since the 'Wings Over the World Tour' more than 12 years earlier. What's more, for the first time a McCartney tour also had a corporate sponsor in the form of Visa, the credit card company. This, like it or not, was the way forward for rock 'n' roll. Almost three years later, in February 1993, with the

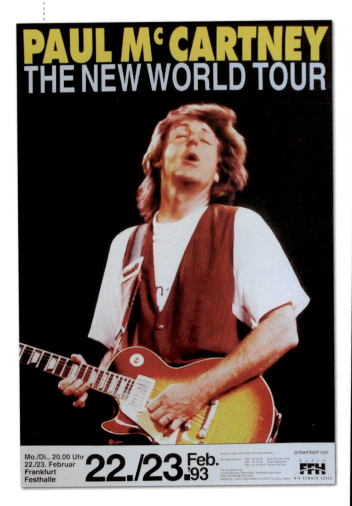

same band line-up apart from Chris Whitten being replaced on drums by Blair Cunningham, the 'New World Tour', sponsored by the German electronics company Grundig, would head across Europe, Australia, New Zealand, North America, South America, Japan and England in support of the *Off the Ground* album released that year.

As before, a tour of such magnitude was a perfect way for Paul and Linda to raise awareness of animal rights issues across the world, but one new aspect of the 'New World Tour' was actually focused on Paul's hometown in an effort to raise money for the Liverpool Institute of Performing Arts (LIPA),

which he had helped to establish back in 1992. He had been visiting the site of his former school, the Liverpool Institute for Boys, in 1988 and was shocked to see the building's state of disrepair following its closure three years earlier. He vowed to help save it and was introduced by George Martin to Mark Featherstone-Witty who had helped set up the Brit School in south London back in 1991. Mark had been putting forward ideas for a performing arts institution of university level in the UK for some time and, together, he and Paul drew up plans for LIPA. Queen Elizabeth II opened LIPA on 7 June 1996 with its first intake of just under 200 students arriving that year. Of its overall cost of £18 million, Paul contributed £3 million and is very proud (and probably relieved) that the institute has proved a huge success over the last 25 years.

Above Right: Paul McCartney portrait taken during the 'New World Tour', Florida, 1993

Chapter 8: 1987-92: Animals, Elvis And Classical Gas

In 1988 Paul and Linda had been persuaded by Linda's new friend Carla Lane to take on cameo roles in an episode of her television comedy series, *Bread*. Set, as always, in Liverpool, where Paul had paid a visit to his old school to take part in a short film about its history, the plot for the episode of *Bread* involved Linda opening an animal rescue centre. During the filming, they became friendly with the leading star of the show, actress Jean Boht who played the mother of the fractured Boswell family, but in real life was married to the well-known American composer and conductor Carl Davis. When Jean and husband Carl paid a visit to Blossom Wood Farm shortly afterwards, Davis asked Paul if he would be interested in collaborating on an orchestral piece of music for the Royal Liverpool Philharmonic to celebrate its 150th anniversary. The piece would be an oratorio, sung by a choir, with a religious theme based on certain aspects of Liverpool history. Paul was immediately intrigued by the idea and keen to take part in what would be another major development in his already remarkable career – his first piece of classical music.

The nearest Paul had come to writing anything 'classical' so far was his largely flute and guitar theme tune for the film soundtrack of *The Family Way* back in 1967, arranged and orchestrated by George Martin. More recent soundtrack work had been the extended version of 'Eleanor Rigby' – 'Eleanor's Dream' – a symphonic instrumental section on *Give My Regards to Broad Street*; on the LP version the 'Dream' section was only just over one minute long, but for the CD the song was extended by more than seven minutes. The lovely baroque melody is certainly Paul's, but again with considerable help from George Martin for the arrangement. Paul had never shown a huge interest in classical music in the past but he took on this considerable commitment seriously over the next two years, meeting with Carl Davis on a regular basis to perform the melodies he'd come up with, which Davis would then notate and orchestrate. It was a slow process and, as always with Paul, there was often tension and disagreements between the two, despite Davis being far more experienced at this kind of composition. Finally completed and rehearsed, the 97-minute long *Liverpool Oratorio* made up of eight loosely autobiographical movements was premiered in front of an audience of 2500 family members, friends and well-known celebrities on 28 June 1991 at Liverpool's Anglican Cathedral; an emotional night for Paul who had auditioned for a place in the cathedral's choir as an 11-year-old schoolboy… and been turned down. Overall the piece and performance were reasonably well-received although, as always, some media reviews leaned towards terms such as "simplistic", "lacklustre" and "insubstantial". For McCartney, nonetheless, it was yet another box ticked; it would be six more years before he'd have another go, with *Standing Stone* in 1997, followed by *Working Classical* in 1999.

There'd be no studio rock album from Paul either until 1997 with the release of one of his best ever, *Flaming Pie*, but there would be a lot of new things, and difficult things, to deal with between now and then.

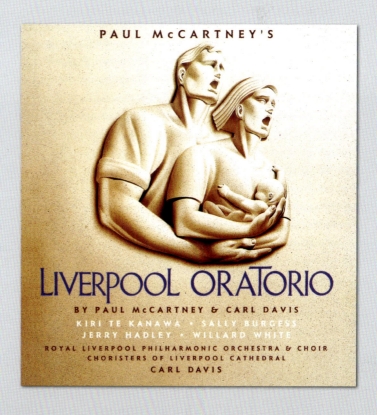

Chapter 9:
1993-99: Fireman With An Hourglass

As if to prove that he wasn't now some fuddy-duddy old codger (he was 50) who only writes oratorios, in 1993 McCartney made yet another move into a completely new field of music – experimental electronic sounds from an unknown (at the time) duo called the Fireman. Paul had finished recording the tracks for *Off the Ground* and wanted some help from another producer in an effort to roughen up the edges that he felt had been smoothed over too much in the production process. Recommended to him by staff at MPL Communications was Youth – actually Martin Glover, a founding member and bass player for the band Killing Joke.

Youth visited Hog Hill Mill Studio and they began remixing the songs for *Off the Ground*, enjoying the process so much that they started working on new material that would eventually become the album *Strawberries Oceans Ships Forest*. Released in November 1993 with no information or band names on the album cover, it nevertheless went down very well and earned several positive media reviews. When someone revealed the true identities of the Fireman, interest increased rapidly. Two more albums would arrive over the next 15 years and there's no doubt the whole concept not only excited Paul and "lent an electricity" to his compositions but also inspired him to look for other collaborators that otherwise might not have taken place – the likes of Nitin Sawhney's *Fluid* EP remixes of tracks from the Fireman's *Rushes*, and DJ Freelance Hellraiser's remixes of various solo McCartney material. Experimentation is something McCartney has always welcomed and embraced.

One more thing needed taking care of in November 1993 with the release of the *Paul is Live* album. Made up of performances from the 'New World Tour', supporting the *Off the Ground* CD released earlier in the year, it proved to be Paul's worst-selling live album so far, largely because ticket sales had fallen way below expectation. Paul, sufficiently disappointed at the results, used it as an opportunity to dismiss his (and Linda's) manager Richard Ogden, despite his dedication and loyalty for the last six years. When he was offered a significant amount of money by a UK Sunday newspaper to tell his side of the story, Ogden commendably turned it down.

Such dedication was equally required from Paul (and George and Ringo) in 1993 when a giant project called *The Beatles Anthology* began to pick up speed. Work had got underway back in 1991 with Apple's chief executive Neil Aspinall organising various elements of what would eventually become an impressive CD boxset, or three triple-albums, released over 11 months, from November 1995 to October 1996. The overall package would also include a television documentary and DVD, plus a large format hardback book, all combining to present a history of the Beatles in more detail than ever before. It would take up a great deal of Paul's time for the next two years, which meant he had no choice other than to disband certainly one of the best groups of

Right: Paul McCartney, Milan, Italy, at the opening show of the 'New World Tour', 1993

Chapter 9: 1993-99: Fireman With An Hourglass   89

Anthology was the first time the three remaining Fab Four had worked so closely for a long time – there was little choice, despite not a huge amount of enthusiasm for the project from Harrison – but by this stage George and Ringo could both do with some additional funds to maintain their rather extravagant lifestyles. Ultimately the project seemed to bring everyone together in a more positive frame of mind than any previous attempts at a reunion. Activities peaked in 1994 when Paul inducted John Lennon into the Rock & Roll Hall of Fame as a solo artist – one of the first to achieve a second nomination. At his speech Paul read out an emotional personal letter he had written to John to bring back memories of their early times together in the Beatles. When Yoko walked onto the stage they embraced in friendship for the first time in years. It was the perfect opportunity for Paul to ask Yoko if there was any material of John's she might have that the other three Beatles could work on together for the Anthology; the result, with help from ELO's Jeff Lynne, was two new John Lennon songs released as Beatles singles – 'Free as a Bird' in December 1995 and 'Real Love' early the next year. They were a fitting way of saying goodbye not only to John but, finally, to the Beatles as well.

The year 1995 had seen many positives for Paul McCartney – both musically and within the family – his daughter, Stella, for one, celebrating her college graduation show as a fashion designer with support from three of the world's top supermodels (Kate Moss, Naomi Campbell and Yasmin Le Bon) taking to

the catwalk (for free) wearing her standout designs. Paul and Linda were, naturally, very proud, as they were of all four of their (despite everything!) well-educated, well-balanced children.

Sadly, 1995 would also bring the sort of news no family ever wants to hear. In December, Linda, now 54, had visited her local GP feeling unwell; two weeks later she was referred to a London specialist who diagnosed breast cancer – the same disease that had taken Paul's mother Mary far too early at the age of just 47. Linda was admitted to the private Princess Grace Hospital in Marylebone, London, where the tumour was removed. Sadly the cancer had already spread to her lymph nodes and she required chemotherapy at a London clinic, Paul staying with her throughout the treatment.

Ringo Starr's first wife Maureen, or Mo, had died in December 1994 at the age of just 48 as a result of leukemia and the sad news that Linda was now fighting breast cancer brought Paul and Ringo closer, spending time playing songs together including the co-written 'Really Love You', as well as 'Beautiful Night' and 'Little Willow', a song Paul had written in memory of Mo; all would appear on the album *Flaming Pie* in 1997. Linda's illness was by now a major news story and the McCartneys continued throughout to reassure everyone that her treatment was going well and they were confident she would make a full recovery. Linda's

L to R: Robbie McIntosh, Wix Wickens, Linda, Paul, Blair Cunningham and Hamish Stuart, September, 1993

Chapter 9: 1993-99: Fireman With An Hourglass

attitude, as expected, would be to prepare for the worst by putting her papers in order, but bravely fighting on in the belief that she could beat her cancer. That was what she intended to do – there was still a lot of life to enjoy.

The McCartney family spent time together back in Scotland where Paul once again purchased more land, this time from neighbours who owned High Ranachan Farm next door; adding its 300 acres to their existing property portfolio in Scotland gave them more than 1000 acres in which to relax and enjoy each other's company in relative peace and quiet. And back in London Paul became Sir Paul McCartney on 11 March 1997 when he was knighted by the Queen at Buckingham Palace for his "services to music", having been nominated by his Liverpool Institute for Performing Arts colleague Mark Featherstone-Witty. Accompanied by three of his children, Mary, Stella and James, Paul quipped, "I would have loved the whole family to be here, but when we heard there were only three tickets, we had to draw straws." And later in his fanzine *Club Sandwich* he commented, "The best thing about it is that when me and Linda are sitting alone on holiday, watching the sunset, I can turn to her and say 'Hey, you're a Lady'. It's a giggle, because you get to make your girl a Lady – although she always was to me anyway."

In truth Linda had not been well enough to attend the ceremony; as the best alternative imaginable she presented her husband with a watch she had bought for him inscribed with the message: "To Paul, my knight in shining armour."

Over the next year the crazy world of Sir Paul McCartney would continue with his usual list of career-defining moments: one of his best ever solo albums *Flaming Pie* was released to considerable acclaim in May 1997, on which Linda, despite her illness, was still able to contribute backing vocals; four months later came his second major classical piece of music, *Standing Stone,* put together with help from the composer David Matthews, which premiered at the Royal Albert Hall in London on 14 October 1997. Linda was able to attend with

Paul and the two sat holding hands as the London Symphony Orchestra played through the piece's 75 minutes towards its moving finale with the 120-member choir singing the words: "*Now, with all the time it seemed we had, whatever time I have to spare, will be with you, for evermore.*"

Despite the best efforts of medical science and the deepest-felt love and prayers from home and abroad, Linda's health was deteriorating. Towards the end of March the McCartneys flew over to their ranch in Tucson where Linda, surrounded by her family, died peacefully on April 17, 1998. A memorial service was held at St Martin's-in-the-Field near Trafalgar Square on 8 June 1998 attended by 700 friends, family and colleagues, including George Harrison, Ringo Starr and Sir George Martin with their wives Olivia, Barbara and Judy. John McGeachy, a piper from Campbeltown who had played on Wings' biggest hit, 'Mull of Kintyre' played the song once again from the St Martin's balcony. Two weeks later a similar memorial event was held in New York for Linda's American family and friends.

It had been a very difficult period for the McCartney family but there were some positive things to celebrate within the next few months, particularly the marriage of their daughter Mary to Alistair Donald, her Rye school friend now working as a film-maker in London. Paul proudly walked her down the aisle of the local church in Peasmarsh in September 1998. And just six months after that happy event, in March 1999, Paul was inducted into the Rock & Roll Hall of Fame for the second time, as a solo artist, catching up at last with his friend, John Lennon. Paul's daughter Stella was with him in New York on the night wearing a bold, white vest; in large capital letters across the front screamed her slogan: 'ABOUT FUCKING TIME !'.

Left: One of the last pictures ever taken of 'The Lovely Linda'

Chapter 10:
1999-2003: Hatches, Matches, Dispatches

The year after Linda's death had not been easy for Paul who struggled to throw himself back into his, as always, overloaded diary of work commitments. Friends and even professional grieving counsellors he had spoken to advised him that work was the best way to diminish the pain he was feeling and, given time, his active life began to reappear. In April 1999 he had been reminded in the happiest of ways that life goes on when his daughter Mary presented him with his first grandchild, Arthur. That same month a concert to mark the first anniversary of Linda's death was held at the Royal Albert Hall with the proceeds going to animal charities. A list of stars lined up to take part including Tom Jones, Elvis Costello, the Pretenders, George Michael and Ladysmith Black Mambazo. Paul hadn't intended to perform himself but eventually changed his mind and brought the show to an end supported by Elvis Costello and the Pretenders, dedicating his set to his wife, his children and his new little grandson. For Paul it was a much-needed turning point in his life.

In typical Paul fashion, just one month after the show, he was attending the *Daily Mirror*'s first 'Pride of Britain Awards' at the Dorchester Hotel in London where he was to present a 'Linda McCartney Award for Animal Welfare'. It was there for the first time that he set eyes upon a young woman who gave a moving speech about the crisis of caring for limb amputees around the world. She herself had lost a leg in 1993 when, at the age of 25, she had been hit by a police motorcyclist while crossing a road in central London. For anyone, but especially for

her working as a fashion model at the time, it was a life-changing moment. Subsequently she founded her own charity to raise money for children injured by landmines in war zones and to improve the NHS's care for amputees in the UK: the Heather Mills Health Trust. Paul and Heather were introduced at the awards event and subsequently he donated £150,000 to her Trust.

By September 1999 Paul and Heather were enjoying a clandestine affair, most of the time in a small cottage Paul owned in Rye. By January 2000 they had attended a party together celebrating Heather's 32nd birthday. The following month she spent 10 days with Paul at Parrot Cay, an exclusive Caribbean resort. By March she had sold her house in Hampshire and bought a new property in Brighton so she would be closer to Rye. The media had started sniffing around and soon there was no point trying to hide it anymore: they were an item. By July 2001 they would be engaged, and a song called 'Heather' would appear on Paul's first solo album for more than four years, *Driving Rain*, along with several other songs dedicated to her including 'Your Loving Flame', 'Riding into Jaipur' (the Indian city where he had purchased Heather's engagement ring), and 'I Do'. By June 2002 they were married. Paul was besotted with an attractive young woman 25 years younger than himself. Some friends and family members by now had already questioned whether

Right: *Paul McCartney and Heather Mills, 2000*

Chapter 10: 1999-2003: Hatches, Matches, Dispatches   95

this was a wise move, but Paul dismissed any such suggestions. For the first time since Linda had died, he was once again a very happy, and very productive man.

In the time between meeting Heather in 1999 and marrying her in 2002 he had put together a second rock 'n' roll covers album, *Run Devil Run*; performed it live at the Cavern in Liverpool with a new band made up of old friends including Pink Floyd's guitarist Dave Gilmour, the Pirates' guitarist Mick Green and Deep Purple's drummer Ian Paice; overseen a history of Wings double album called *Wingspan* with an accompanying TV documentary; released his second classical album *Working Classical* and started work on his third, *Ecce Cor Meum,* for the opening of Oxford University Magdalen College's new concert hall; and a sort of ambient/classical/mash-up compilation called *Liverpool Sound Collage,* put together for his friend Peter Blake's art exhibition being held in their hometown.

Paul could never be happier than when busy – even that busy – but, as always, some rather sad events weren't far away. In March 2000 Paul heard the shocking news that Linda's first husband, Mel See, suffering from severe depression, had taken his own life at his home in Tucson at the age of 62. Then, in 2001, just four months after Paul and Heather had got engaged, George Harrison died at the age of 58 as the result of throat cancer – the same illness that had taken Derek Taylor, press officer for the Beatles and Apple Corps, four years earlier at the age of 65.

Before George passed away, Paul and Ringo were able to pay him a visit at a hotel room in New York where he was being cared for. The three remaining Beatles talked about their lives together and shared a few tears but, according to medical staff attending, a lot more laughter than tears. Paul arranged for George to spend his last few days at the McCartney home in Los Angeles. It was there that George died on 29

November 2001 with his family – wife Olivia and son Dhani – and a number of close associates by his side, including his teacher and lifelong friend, Indian sitar player Ravi Shankar. When hearing of George's death, Paul said: "He was a lovely guy and a very brave man and had a wonderful sense of humour. He is really just my baby brother."

As if those personal losses weren't enough for anyone, it had been on 11 September 2001 that Paul and Heather were sitting on an airplane at John F. Kennedy Airport in New York about to fly back to London when the worst possible thing imaginable took place – the terrorist attacks on the Twin Towers. The McCartneys returned to their Long Island home for a few days before Heather made a suggestion that Paul should organise a charity concert to raise money for the victims of 9/11. Paul wasn't sure that was a good idea as his new album, *Driving Rain*, was about to be released just two months later and some might think he was using the tragedy as a way to promote his record. In the end he wrote a song (with Heather) called 'Freedom' and agreed to take part in promoter Harvey Weinstein's concert televised by VH-1, elevated to the headlining spot. The 'Concert for New York' took place on 20 October 2001 at the Madison Square Garden where some of the biggest stars in the world – David Bowie, Elton John, Billy Joel, Bon Jovi, Jay-Z, Mick Jagger and Keith Richards, Eric Clapton and Buddy Guy, Destiny's Child, the Who and many others – performed in support of the New York City Fire and Police Departments and the families of the almost 3000 people who had so tragically lost their lives on 9/11.

With *Driving Rain* released three weeks later, Paul had his own extensive list of concerts coming up over the next year: the 'Driving World Tour' in 2002 taking in North America, Mexico and Japan; and the 'Back in the World Tour' a year later travelling across Western and Eastern Europe, including Russia. All were to feature McCartney's

Chapter 10: 1999-2003: *Hatches, Matches, Dispatches*

new band with an almost entirely revised line-up apart from Paul 'Wix' Wickens on keyboards; he was joined by three top notch American session players – Rusty Anderson on guitar, Brian Ray on guitar and bass, and Abe Laboriel Jr. on drums. All four continue to perform with Paul to this day. Two live albums were released from the tours: *Back in the US: Live 2002* and *Back in the World: Live 2003*.

As for his personal life, as 2002 got underway, everything seemed to be running smoothly. For Heather he had bought a new seaside home near Brighton, at a cost of £800,000 and advanced another £150,000 to decorate and furnish it. She accompanied Paul to New Orleans in February where he performed his 9/11 tribute song 'Freedom' at the US Super Bowl XXXVI, before setting off on the 'Driving World Tour' in April, spending over 10 months performing 58 shows. Heather was there virtually the entire time, and everything appeared to be a love-in tour for all concerned. Behind the scenes, however, it was far different. Arguments, serious arguments, were being heard on an increasingly regular basis. One evening Paul threw Heather's very expensive engagement ring from the hotel balcony into the garden below, shouting "The wedding's off!" Staff had to use metal detectors to help them eventually find it.

Back home in the UK media there had already been suggestions that Heather Mills was not the person Paul seemed to think (or had thought) she was. Some implied that her career as a model was perhaps not quite the sort of model she had implied. Several years before, after her terrible accident with the police motorcycle, she had published a book called *Out on a Limb,* which included graphic descriptions of her upbringing by a violent father; of being kidnapped at the age of eight by a swimming instructor; that she had run away from home to live with a boy from a travelling fair; that she had spent time homeless living on the streets of London. People who had known her at that stage in her life began to come forward to say that little of what she claimed was true. Her first husband also appeared on the scene claiming that throughout their relationship Heather had been a compulsive liar.

Paul had friends who from the outset had not liked Heather at all, finding her unfriendly and aloof. Some even thought they had come across her in the past and described her as an attractive girl out in the Soho clubs on a regular basis in an attempt to snare a sugar daddy. It might not be true, of course, but there's no doubt that was exactly what she had achieved, and a good one, at that. The richest musician in the world. But at that stage they still weren't married. The wedding wasn't due to take place until June. There was still time to get out of it... He didn't. A break in the 'Driving World Tour' allowed them to return from the USA and for Paul to appear in a concert on 3 June 2002 at Buckingham Palace, celebrating the Queen's 50 years on the throne. Eight days later, on 11 June, Paul and Heather were married at a ceremony in St. Salvator's Church in County Monaghan, Ireland – the part of Ireland where his mother Mary had been born.

A guest list of 300 friends and family attended the wedding and a wonderful time was had by all. Sort of. All of Paul's children attended the wedding although there were plenty of rumours going around that none of them were very happy about it. Stella would get married on the Isle of Bute just over two months later, to Alasdhair Willis, a creative director and brand consultant whom she had met at a business meeting in 2001. They have now been happily married for 20 years and have four children. For Sir Paul and his new Lady McCartney, however, marital happiness would not last long. Chaos and creation were just around the corner. Creation saw the birth of their baby Beatrice on 28 October 2003. Chaos took a different form altogether.

Epilogue:
2003-23: Chaos And Creation

In 2003 Paul told his office to contact Michael Eavis – the founder of what's considered by many to be the best music and arts festival in the world – to see if he could perform on the main Pyramid Stage that year. He'd left it too late – they'd already booked Radiohead – but Eavis was quick to point out they'd be very happy to offer Paul the headlining Saturday night slot for the following year. Perfect. A short foreign excursion of 14 shows across Western and Eastern Europe, known as the '04 Summer Tour', would come to an end on Saturday 26 June with McCartney's first ever performance at Glastonbury. It was one of the few occasions Paul was genuinely nervous when he took a look at the 100,000-plus Pyramid Stage audience, but it proved to be regarded as one of his best ever shows – two and a half hours of Beatles, Wings and solo music that left the audience in rapture and, backstage, McCartney and Eavis both in tears. No surprise that he's now played there three times – returning in 2014 and again in 2022.

There was no album to promote at Glastonbury but that didn't matter. Outdoor concerts were the place to be. In February 2005 he would perform at Super Bowl XXXIX – his second appearance at the event in three years (unheard of) – and in July that year he also took the final slot at the Live 8 benefit concert at London's Hyde Park, despite all four members of Pink Floyd playing together for the first (and last) time in 24 years. He then headed off on yet another two-month trip to the States for the rather unimaginably titled 'US Tour', kicking off in Miami on 17 September, five days after the release of *Chaos and Creation in the Backyard*.

But after creation came chaos. By this stage, Paul's marriage to Heather was crumbling. They were spending more time now in the USA than the UK, thanks to his regular tours and Heather's desire to live in the Big Apple rather than a farm in East Sussex, especially one full of pictures and memories of Linda. Paul was in the process of building a new lodge-style home for them on Woodlands Farm, part of his East Sussex estate now approaching 1000 acres after regularly buying as much adjacent land to Blossom Wood Farm as he could find. He'd also bought an apartment in Manhattan, which provided offices for the American arm of MPL Communications and a penthouse suite on the top floor. When Heather said she wanted her own office at the same location, Paul said that wasn't possible but found suitable premises nearby. She was furious. Despite Paul providing her with the house in Brighton, a flat in London, an open credit card and an annual allowance worth £360,000 as well as a succession of expensive gifts, nothing ever seemed to be quite enough for Lady McCartney. When Paul discovered she had contacted MPL's accountants in London and asked them to pay £450,000 into her bank account to pay off the mortgage on her London flat, enough was enough: there was no mortgage on the flat, it had already been paid for. When she made the same request again in 2006, their marriage by then had drifted onto the rocks. Within two months they had separated.

Right: *Paul McCartney performs at the Coachella Music and Arts Festival at the Empire Polo Field on April 17, 2009 in Palm Desert, California*

Epilogue: 2003-2023: Chaos And Creation

Despite claims in a joint statement that their "parting is an amicable one and both of us still care about each other very much", such warm feelings did not last long. On 29 July Paul took out divorce proceedings on the grounds of Heather's "unreasonable behaviour" and her refusal to have sex with him. Her response accused Paul of being "controlling and possessive" with regular displays of violent and drunken behaviour. The War of the McCartneys had been declared and would continue until peace broke out almost two years later. The media, of course, loved every second, with the legal proceedings and arguments gaining more coverage than any divorce case since Prince Charles and Princess Diana back in 1996 – indeed, the solicitors representing Paul and Heather were the same as those who had performed the same role for the royal couple...To start with, at least.

The first preliminary hearing was held on 27 February 2007 with Heather asking for a £50 million settlement; Paul offered £16.5 million plus the properties he'd already paid for while with her, bringing the total up to £20 million. She rejected the offer... and on and on it went, increasing in unpleasant tackiness on a daily basis. By the time the case actually made it to court, Heather was now representing herself (having fallen out with her lawyers) and her settlement request had risen to £125 million! Many of her claims were nothing short of ridiculous. Thankfully, Paul's lawyers, and the judge, saw through them as a tissue of lies. The judge, Mr. Justice Hugh Bennett, found in Paul's favour, reducing her payment to £14 million plus £2.5 million to purchase a new home – basically the £16.5 million Paul had offered back in 2007. Paul also agreed to pay for his daughter's school fees and a nanny, as well as a £35,000 a year fund for Beatrice herself.

Neither Paul, and certainly not Heather, had come out of this divorce very well – who ever does? – but there was no doubt Paul was the winner, especially when the judge read out his decision on 17 March 2008, referring to Paul as: "balanced" and "consistent, accurate and honest".

Heather, not so. He said: "I am driven to the conclusion that much of her evidence, both written and oral, was not just inconsistent and inaccurate but also less than candid. Overall, she was a less than impressive witness." Much of what she had said, he concluded, was "typical of her make believe". He issued a decree nisi on 8 May 2008, which would become final after a period of six months separation. The war was over.

For all involved it had been a difficult two years but for Paul there were positives to soften the blow. In June 2007 his album *Memory Almost Full* was his first to be released by Hear Music, a record label founded that year as a partnership between Concord Music Group and coffeehouse giant Starbucks, with McCartney as their first-signed artist. The album was generally very well-received by the media and public, achieving Top 5 status in UK and US charts. A series of just six 'secret' shows took place in relatively small venues to promote the album – three in London, and one each in New York, Los Angeles and Paris.

At the end of the tour Paul had started dating an attractive and wealthy New Jersey woman called Nancy Shevell, the daughter of a trucking magnate of whose company she was the Vice President; she also lived in the area of Long Island known as the Hamptons. Paul was introduced to Nancy, aged 48 at the time, by her second cousin, the TV news presenter Barbara Walters, who felt they would get on very well; both were going through difficult divorces at the time. (They got engaged on 6 May 2011, and married five months later on 9 October at Marylebone Registry Office in London, where Paul had married Linda in 1969. Sometimes the simple option is the best option. His seven-year-old daughter Beatrice was the bridesmaid; brother Mike, for the third time, his best man.)

One sad event just after Paul's divorce had been settled was the death of the Beatles' old school friend, tour manager and subsequent head of Apple Corps, Neil Aspinall, who died

Epilogue: 2003-2023: Chaos And Creation   101

Above: Paul and Heather Mills McCartney arrive at the 'Adopt-A-Minefield' Benefit Gala in support of landmines victims. May 28, 2005 in Neuss, Germany

of lung cancer in New York on 24 March 2008 at the age of 66. His funeral took place in Twickenham, southwest London (the town where the early 'Get Back' recording sessions had taken place in 1969); many Beatles associates attended, but not Paul, or Ringo. Paul had visited Neil in New York not long before he died to say goodbye and had also covered Neil's substantial medical costs. Funerals were still not Paul's thing.

Above: Paul McCartney performs onstage at the Hollywood Bowl on March 30, 2010

Above Right: Paul McCartney and his new wife Nancy Shevell leave London's Marylebone registry office on their wedding day, 9th October 2011

Concerts, thankfully, still were and still are. That year he returned to Liverpool to celebrate its status as the European Capital of Culture with a concert held on 1 June 2008 at Anfield, home of Liverpool Football Club. Over 36,000 attended a very moving night in Paul's hometown, which he described as "the city of culture in the centre of the universe". That went down very well. Most of those in the stadium were local Liverpudlians who left the stadium in a similar mood to when one of the city's football clubs win a big match – but there were plenty of other special guests among them, including Sir George Martin and two American women who seemed to enjoy the show even more. Yoko Ono and Olivia Harrison sat singing along in the city where their husbands had started their amazing journeys back in 1960. A few tears were shed when Paul performed George's 'Something' on a ukulele, and the Beatles' 'A Day in the Life' segued into a moving rendition of John's 'Give Peace a Chance'.

On the night, Paul was one year past his 'When I'm Sixty-Four' ditty, one of the first songs he ever wrote as a teenager; he was 65 - retirement age - with 66 just a couple of weeks away, but there was certainly no sign of him giving up his chosen career. There was more than enough on the horizon to keep Sir Paul McCartney busy over the next 15 years.

His third collaboration with Martin Glover, the Fireman, saw them release their third album together in 2008, *Electric Arguments,* to great acclaim, making it the first of their work to make it into the UK and US charts. Three more tours got underway in July of 2009 - 'Summer Live '09' took in nine shows across America including three nights as the first band to perform at Citi Field, the new home of the New York Mets baseball team, eventually released as a live album *Good Evening New York City* in 2009. The 'Good Evening Europe Tour' took them through to Christmas 2009, followed by the much grander 'Up and Coming Tour' taking in North and South America, plus seven shows covering the UK and Ireland, including his first ever performance at the Isle of Wight Festival on 13

Epilogue: 2003-2023: Chaos And Creation   103

June 2010. On top of that, Paul received the Library of Congress' Gershwin Prize for Popular Song from President Barack Obama on 2 June before performing to a star-studded audience at the White House, joined on stage by Stevie Wonder to perform 'Ebony and Ivory'.

The 'On the Run Tour' got underway in July 2011, again taking in Europe and North and South America playing 37 shows. His fifth classical album *Ocean's Kingdom*, commissioned by the New York Ballet, came out in October 2011 followed by yet another covers album early in 2012 – the rather curiously entitled *Kisses on the Bottom* (lyrics from a Fats Waller song) featuring a selection of old traditional jazz numbers that Paul as a boy would often hear his father perform on the piano. Stevie Wonder played harmonica on one song, Eric Clapton guitar on a couple more, while a collection of top jazz musicians including Diana Krall, John Pizzarelli and Christian McBride added their talents to the album's overall sense of coolness. Another Top 5 hit in the UK/US charts.

In June 2012 Paul headlined the Queen's Diamond Jubilee Concert held outside Buckingham Palace, and a month later topped the opening ceremony of the 2012 London Olympics. By this stage he was already working on his next studio album, *New*, which would arrive in the shops in October 2013. And what does McCartney do when he's got a new album out? ... He goes on tour – his biggest since 1989, the 'Out There Tour' taking in 91 shows across 19 countries spread over two-and-a-half years. Yes, there were four-month breaks from Christmas to March each year, but it's still a pretty impressive commitment for a man who was 70 when the tour started, and 73 when it reached the end. You begin to wonder, is there more than one Paul McCartney?

And on it continues... In 2014 he gave his second stunning performance on Glastonbury's Pyramid Stage and also that year took up rap as a new hobby, collaborating with American Kanye West on the single 'Only One', in 2015 with West and Rihanna on the single 'FourFiveSeconds', and later that year on West's follow-up single 'All Day' with rappers Theophilus London and Allan Kingdom.

In 2016 he released *Pure McCartney*, a career-spanning collection of solo material from Wings all the way through to the Fireman. Before it was even released he'd set off on another huge tour, 'One on One' spread over 20 months, taking in all the usual countries but throwing in Australia and New Zealand, where he hadn't played since 1993. He had, however, paid a visit to Australia in 2015 for filming his cameo role in the fifth episode of *Pirates of the Caribbean: Dead Men Tell No Tales*, released in 2017. Performing as the character Uncle Jack, he plays cards in a Caribbean prison waiting for his own execution, singing an old traditional folk song, 'Maggie Mae' - a raucous tale about a Liverpool prostitute that first appears on the Beatles' album *Let it Be* back in 1970.

On 26 July 2018, Paul played once again at the Cavern Club, at the age of 76, with his now regular and very well-seasoned band. The show was filmed and eventually broadcast by the BBC on Christmas Day 2020, as *Paul McCartney: Live at the Cavern Club*. In 2018 he also released his studio album *Egypt Station* having returned once more to Capitol Records - his first album in 36 years to make it to No. 1 in the US Billboard charts since *Tug of War*, and to No. 3 in the UK. Just 10 days after its release he set off on yet another tour to promote the album, 'Freshen Up' - 39 shows over 10 months in North and South America, Europe and Japan. There would have been more, but Covid-19 arrived and a series of shows in Europe had to be cancelled, including his third appearance at Glastonbury. Instead of putting his feet up he took the

opportunity to work on his third genuine solo album (apart from minor additions by band members on one track), *McCartney III*, released in December 2020. In the charts it did even better than *Egypt Station*, making it to No. 1 in the UK and No. 2 in the USA.

Enough, you might say, but there's more. In November 2021 his book *The Lyrics: 1956 to the Present* was released, based on conversations Paul had with the Irish poet Paul Muldoon. It went on to win 'Book of the Year' awards from both Waterstones in the UK and Barnes & Noble in the USA. Nice to add to his *Hey Grandude!* and *Grandude's Green Submarine* children's books published by Puffin in 2019 and 2021. They didn't win any awards but, come on, by this time he had eight grandchildren! And they really had come up with the name Grandude.

McCartney's 'Got Back Tour', his most recent and last to date, ran from April to June 2022 taking in 16 shows in the States before returning to the UK for his third performance at Glastonbury, making up for the show being cancelled two years earlier. The night before Saturday's headlining slot he performed a sort of warm-up gig at the small market town of Frome, just a few miles from Glastonbury, as part of the annual Frome Festival. The 800 tickets were snapped up in minutes when the secret gig was revealed that morning.

Why he needed a warm-up after almost two months of live shows in the USA is a good question, but maybe, even after more than 60 years of performing on stage, he was still a little nervous. Glastonbury is huge, the Pyramid Stage audience can reach well over 100,000 cider-drinking festival-goers, and he had just turned the age of 80 a week before. He had every right to be nervous, but he didn't need to be. At around 9.30pm he walked on stage and became the oldest solo headliner at Glastonbury Festival ever. Yes, even older than Bruce Springsteen, who joined him on stage to sing 'Glory Days' and 'I Wanna Be Your Man'. At the end, Springsteen and the Foo Fighter's Dave Grohl joined him to play the

Epilogue: 2003-2023: *Chaos And Creation*

classic *Abbey Road* medley: 'Golden Slumbers', 'Carry That Weight', and 'The End'. 1969. Once upon a long ago.

The three-hour set was a stormer, the crowd seemed to love every minute, and at one point let him know how they felt by singing 'Happy Birthday'. A lot of people believe he owns that song; he doesn't. He might wish he does, but that didn't bother him too much. What he was, quite clearly, was touched.

After the show he celebrated his 80th birthday backstage until the early hours with friends and family, including his wife, some of his children and even a few of his eight grandchildren. It was a late night for them, but they got it right: he is a pretty cool Grandude! One of the greatest musicians the world has ever known. Many predicted his headlining performance at Glastonbury 2022, at the age of 80, would be his last live concert... In October 2023 the 'Got Back Tour' gets underway once again in Australia, Mexico and Brazil. Just another tour, just another day, for Sir Paul McCartney.

A week after turning 80, Paul headlines the Pyramid Stage at Glastonbury Festival for the third time. June 25, 2022

Biographies

Biographies of paul mccartney and the top wings band members and recording/touring musicians, organised chronologically in the order they performed with him.

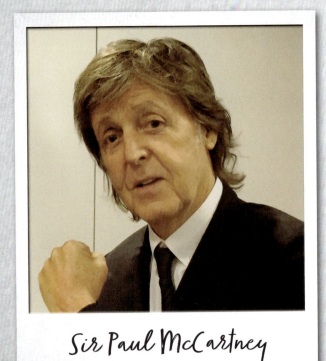

Sir Paul McCartney

Born: 18 June 1942

Place of birth: Liverpool, England

Musical background: Inspired by his father Jim, a pianist, trumpet player and bandleader of Jim Mac's Jazz Band in the Twenties, Paul initially took up the trumpet himself; he soon gave it up because he wanted to be able to sing at the same time as playing, so switched to the guitar and piano. Apart from his father he was strongly influenced by Buddy Holly, Chuck Berry and, in particular, Little Richard. In 1957, at the age of 15, he joined John Lennon's skiffle band the Quarrymen... and the rest is history.

Played on: Everything!

Where is he now? Still songwriting, still performing, still recording and still inspiring young musicians and music fans all around the world. His main place of residence in the UK is in Peasmarsh, near Rye, on the East Sussex border with Kent, but he also has homes in London, Scotland, Los Angeles, New York and a ranch in Tucson, Arizona.

His most important musicians throughout his 50+ year solo career

Linda McCartney

Born: 24 September 1941

Place of birth: Scarsdale, New York, USA

Musical background: Linda began her career as a photographer in the mid-'60s, specialising in images of rock musicians as unofficial house photographer at the famous Fillmore East music venue in New York. On 15 May 1967, while on a photo

Linda McCartney

Where is she now? Apart from her career as a photographer and musician, Linda became a devoted animal rights activist, went on to write several vegetarian cookbooks and with Paul founded the company 'Linda McCartney Foods' in 1991. Sadly, Linda was diagnosed with breast cancer in 1995 and died from the illness on 17 April 1998 at their home in Tucson, Arizona, at the age of just 56.

Sir George Martin

Born: 3 January 1926

Place of birth: Highbury, London, England

Musical background: Born into humble circumstances in north London – his father a carpenter, his mother a cook – the family acquired a piano when George was six years old and he largely taught himself to play. Attending Bromley Grammar School in south London and influenced by the likes of British jazz pianist George Shearing and boogie-woogie American pianist Meade Lux Lewis, George began performing as a young teenager for the local band the Four Tune Tellers. After World War II and his service in the Royal Navy, George trained at the Guildhall School of Music and Drama in London. Encouraged by his teacher and broadcaster Sidney Harrison, George became interested in classical composers including Ravel and Rachmaninoff but also songwriters such as Cole Porter. He also learned the oboe and took up courses in composition and orchestration. He joined EMI in 1950 as assistant to Oscar Preuss, the head of EMI's Parlophone Records for over 30 years. When Preuss retired in 1955, George took over the label… and the rest, once again, is history.

assignment in London, she met Paul McCartney for the first time at a Georgie Fame concert in the Bag O'Nails club. Linda began to learn the piano following the Beatles' split in 1970 and recorded with Paul for the first time on keyboards on Wings' album *Wild Life* in 1971, having previously provided backing vocals on the Beatles' *Let it Be* and Paul's first solo LP *McCartney* in 1970, and their joint recording of *Ram* in 1971. Linda went on to perform with Paul consistently in concert and in the studio through to the 'New World Tour' in 1993 and the album *Flaming Pie* in 1997.

Played on: *McCartney, Ram, Wild Life, Red Rose Speedway, Live and Let Die, Band on the Run, Venus and Mars, Wings at the Speed of Sound, London Town, Back to the Egg, McCartney II, Tug of War, Pipes of Peace, Give My Regards to Broad Street, Press to Play, Flowers in the Dirt, Off the Ground* and *Flaming Pie*. Also performed on the live LPs *Wings Over America, Tripping the Live Fantastic, Unplugged (The Official Bootleg),* and *Paul is Live.*

Sir George Martin

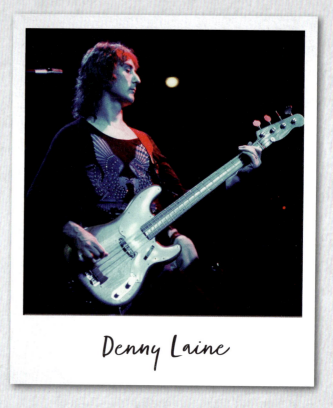

Denny Laine

Played on: *The Family Way*, *Live and Let Die*, *Tug of War*, *Pipes of Peace*, *Give My Regards to Broad Street* and *Flaming Pie*.

Where is he now? Sir George had suffered with stomach cancer for some time and, at the age of 90, died at his home in Wiltshire on 8 March 2016. A memorial service was held on 11 May at St Martin-in-the-Fields, Trafalgar Square, attended by Sir Paul McCartney, Ringo Starr, John and George's wives Yoko Ono and Olivia Harrison, Sir Elton John, and many family members, friends and former colleagues. A fitting tribute in recognition of the work and genius of the genuine 'Fifth Beatle'.

Denny Laine

Born: 29 October 1944

Place of birth: Tyseley, Birmingham, England

Musical background: Born Brian Frederick Hines (a name he changed when forming his first professional band, Denny Laine and the Diplomats), Laine took up guitar at an early age inspired by the gypsy guitarist Django Reinhardt, and went on to become a founder member of the Moody Blues in 1964. He left the group in October 1966 to perform for various other bands and as a solo artist/songwriter. Successful compositions included 'Say You Don't Mind' (a Top 20 hit for Colin Blunstone in 1972). Denny was also a founder member of Wings in 1971 and stayed with the band through to its conclusion.

Played on: *Wild Life*, *Red Rose Speedway*, *Live and Let Die*, *Band on the Run*, *Venus and Mars*, *Wings At the Speed of Sound*, *London Town*, *Back to the Egg*, *Tug of War* and *Pipes of Peace*. Also performed on the live LP *Wings Over America*.

Where is he now? Laine moved to the New Jersey region on the East Coast of the USA in the mid-'90s, where he continues to perform with his own Denny Laine Band.

Denny Seiwell

Born: 10 July 1943

Place of birth: Lehighton, Pennsylvania, USA

Musical background: After learning to play drums while at Lehighton High School, Denny became a member of the original local Carbon County Band formed in 1961. He then enlisted for the US Navy as a musician and played in the Navy Band, based in Washington.

Played on: *Ram*, *Wild Life*, *Red Rose Speedway*, *Live and Let Die* and *Ram On*.

Where is he now? As well as being a founder member of Wings (from whom he resigned in 1973 following disagreements with McCartney), Denny played for the likes of Billy Joel and Liza Minnelli and also performed as a session musician on a number of well-known US film, TV soundtracks and theme tunes. He has lived in Los Angeles since 1975.

Henry McCullough

Born: 21 July 1943

Place of birth: Portstewart, County Londonderry, Northern Ireland

Musical background: Henry's love of music began when at an early age he regularly watched his mother's church choir perform. As a

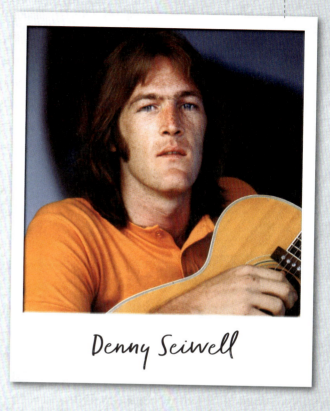

Denny Seiwell

young teenager he joined a well-known Northern Irish showband, the Skyrockets, on lead guitar. In 1967 he moved to Belfast and joined People, who moved to London and were signed by Jimi Hendrix's manager, Chas Chandler, under a new name, Eire Apparent. Jimi Hendrix produced and played on their one and only LP, *Sunrise*, and the band toured with the likes of Pink Floyd, the Move, Soft Machine and the Animals, as well as with the Jimi Hendrix Experience. In 1969 Henry joined the Grease Band as lead guitarist for Joe Cocker's backing band, performing at the Woodstock Festival. In 1970 he played lead guitar on one of the world's most successful rock operas, *Jesus Christ Superstar*. Paul invited Henry to join Wings in 1972.

Played on: *Red Rose Speedway* and *Live and Let Die*.

Where is he now? Henry joined Wings in time to take part in their tour of UK universities and then played on all of their singles that year, as well as their second LP, *Red Rose Speedway*, for which he is best known for the superb, improvised guitar solo on the hit song *My Love*. He left Wings in 1973 just before the sessions for *Band on the Run* got underway. Henry's career continued as a solo and session musician through to 2012 when he suffered a heart attack, from which he never fully recovered. He died at his home in Ballymoney, Northern Ireland, in 2016.

Jimmy McCulloch

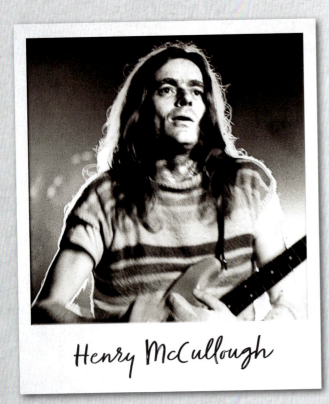

Henry McCullough

Jimmy McCulloch

Born: 4 June 1953

Place of birth: Dumbarton, Scotland

Musical background: Jimmy started playing guitar at the age of 11, also inspired, along with his bandmate Denny Laine, by Django Reinhardt. He made his first performance as guitarist for the Jaygars, later called One in a Million, who supported the Who during their 1967 tour of Scotland. His family moved to London when Jimmy was 13 and he joined the band Thunderclap Newman in 1969. They enjoyed a UK No. 1 hit with 'Something in the Air' that year, which went on to feature in several film soundtracks including the 1969 movies *The Magic Christian* (starring Ringo Starr) and *Easy Rider*. He went on to play with John Mayall and the Bluesbreakers and the Scottish blues-rock band Stone the Crows before joining Wings in August 1974.

Played on: *Venus and Mars*, *Wings at the Speed of Sound* and *London Town*. Also performed on the live LP *Wings Over America*.

Where is he now? Jimmy left Wings in September 1977 after (yet again) disagreements with McCartney but, on this occasion, mainly due to

Jimmy's unacceptable behaviour and drink/drugs problems. He went on to join the Small Faces for one album before becoming a founder member of the band Wild Horses. He was with the band for less than a year and joined the Dukes in 1979 for a short period. He was found dead by his brother, Jack, at his flat in London in September that year. The cause of death was heart failure as a result of drug and alcohol overdoses. He was just 26 years old.

Geoff Britton

Born: 1 August 1943

Place of birth: Lewisham, London, England

Musical background: Geoff was initially inspired by the American jazz drummer Gene Krupa and in his early teens was bought his first drum kit by his mother. In 1970 he joined the Bristol jazz-influenced band East of Eden, playing on their second album *Snafu*. He went on to join the Fifties rock and roll band the Wild Angels before joining Wings in 1974.

Played on: *Venus and Mars*.

Where is he now? Despite his huge respect for Paul McCartney, Geoff left Wings early in 1975 following (you guessed it!) personal disagreements. He joined Rough Diamond in 1977 before Manfred Mann's Earth Band (1978 to '79) and the Keys (1979 to '83). He is a keen fitness and martial arts enthusiast and ran a kickboxing school in London, competing as a Great Britain coach until the early '80s. He moved to Spain in 1989, where he opened a martial arts club, and joined various bands including the Rockets, Major Blues and Angel Station. At the age of 80, Geoff continues to live in Spain where he still plays drums and follows a regular fitness regime.

Geoff Britton

Joe English

Born: 7 February 1949

Place of birth: Rochester, New York, USA

Musical background: Joe took up drums at an early age and was a founder member of the local band Jam Factory, which evolved into the Tall Dogs Orchestra of Macon. In early 1975 he answered an ad for a drummer, not realising it was for Wings. He was employed to replace Geoff Britton during the recording sessions for *Venus and Mars*.

Played on: *Venus and Mars, Wings at the Speed of Sound* and *London Town*. Also performed on the live LP *Wings Over America*.

Where is he now? In 1977 he became ill and homesick and returned to Macon, Georgia, where he began playing with Chuck Leavell (former keyboard player with the Allman Brothers Band and music director for the Rolling Stones since 1982) as the drummer in his band Sea Level. Joe later became a born again Christian and formed the Joe English Band, touring the world with other well-known Christian performers. Unfortunately he has been unable to play drums professionally since the late 1990s, due to chronic problems with his ankles. In 1990 he joined the Word of Faith Fellowship in North Carolina where he continues to be involved in Christian music projects.

Steve Holley

Joe English

Steve Holley

Born: 24 August 1954

Place of birth: West London, England

Musical background: Steve's father, Jeffrey, led a swing band; his mother, Irene, was the singer. His musical training began with the piano, but he took up the drums when he was 12 years old. He worked primarily as a session player (recording with the likes of Joe Cocker, Elton John and Kiki Dee) but also recorded an album with the band Horse. It was in 1978 that, by chance, he bumped into Denny Laine in a pub in Staines, Surrey, and was invited to join Wings.

Played on: *Back to the Egg*. Also played with McCartney's supergroup Rockestra on the fund-raising live album *Concerts for the People of Kampuchea*.

Where is he now? After Wings disbanded Holley continued as a session drummer and, from 1986 to '88, was a member of the US rock band Reckless Sleepers. Since the early 2000s he has been touring with Ian Hunter (Mott the Hoople) as a member of Hunter's Rant Band. He also released a solo album, *The Reluctant Dog*, in 2003.

Laurence Juber

Born: 12 November 1952

Place of birth: Stepney, east London, England

Musical background: A very talented musician inspired by the Beatles in the early '60s, Laurence took up guitar at the age of 10. He was playing semi-professionally by the time he was 13 and went on to study classical guitar at the age of 15. He joined the National Youth Jazz Orchestra and took a music degree at Goldsmiths College in southeast London, studying guitar and lute. He then began his career as a successful session guitarist, playing on a wide variety of well-known albums and film soundtracks. He was invited to join Wings in 1978.

Played on: *Back to the Egg*. Also played with McCartney's supergroup Rockestra on the fund-raising live album *Concerts for the People of Kampuchea*.

Laurence Juber

Where is he now? When Wings disbanded in 1981 Laurence moved to America and made his home in California, where he continues to work as a very successful session musician. He has worked on music for a range of US TV shows, and also recorded with the likes of Belinda Carlisle and Al Stewart, as well as more than 25 solo albums.

Howie Casey

Born: 12 July 1937

Place of birth: Liverpool, England

Musical background: British rock saxophonist who came to prominence in the Sixties with the band Derry and the Seniors – the first rock 'n' roll band from Liverpool to play in Germany and pave the way for the Beatles, whom he met many times. The band later changed its name to Howie Casey and the Seniors and became the first Liverpool band to record an album. He had previously played in a military band while serving his National Service from 1955 and been inspired by Little Richard and Fats Domino. Having become a session player in the Seventies and working with T. Rex, Howie was reintroduced to McCartney by the producer and arranger Tony Visconti to work on *Band on the Run*.

Played on: *Band on the Run, Wings at the Speed of Sound* and *Back to the Egg*. Also performed on the live LP *Wings Over America* and with McCartney's supergroup Rockestra on the fund-raising live album *Concerts for the People of Kampuchea*.

Where is he now? Continues to perform as a session player and has also played with a Beatles/Wings tribute show. He put together his own tribute

Howie Casey

band called Beatles with Wings, who have continued to perform as recently as 2022. Now 85, Howie lives in Bournemouth, Dorset, on the south coast of England.

David Gilmour

Born: 6 March 1946

Place of birth: Cambridge, England

Musical background: Guitarist with Pink Floyd since 1967, Dave was inspired by Bill Haley, Elvis Presley and the Everly Brothers in the Fifties and took up guitar as a result. While at school in Cambridge he met the future Pink Floyd members Syd Barrett and Roger Waters. Also a huge fan of the Beatles, Dave and Paul McCartney have been friends since the Sixties.

Played on: *Back to the Egg*, *Give My Regards to Broad Street*, *Flowers in the Dirt* and *Run Devil Run*. Also played with Wings and McCartney's supergroup Rockestra on the fund-raising live album *Concerts for the People of Kampuchea*.

Where is he now? One of the two remaining original members of Pink Floyd (with Nick Mason), Dave has devoted most of his time over the last few years to his solo career but also as a sideman for a number of artists, often supporting various charities to raise considerable amounts of money. He lives north of Worthing, West Sussex, in the south of England.

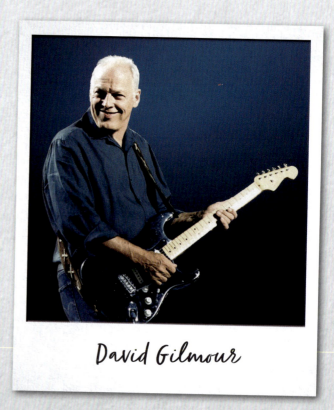

David Gilmour

Biographies   115

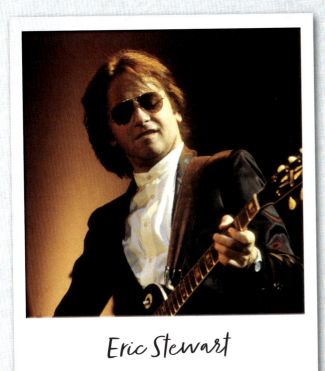

Eric Stewart

Eric Stewart

Born: 20 January 1945

Place of birth: Manchester, England

Musical background: A multi-instrumentalist, Eric grew up influenced by early American guitarists such as Scotty Moore (with Elvis Presley) and James Burton (with Rick Nelson), and later the Beatles and the revered guitar maestro Ry Cooder. He became a founder member of the Mindbenders (with Wayne Fontana) completely by chance when the band auditioned for Fontana Records at a club in Manchester in 1963 and their guitarist didn't turn up; Eric stood in and got the job. The Mindbenders split up in 1968 and Eric invested along with the band's bass player, Graham Gouldman, in a new recording studio in Stockport. The pair later linked up with Lol Crème and Kevin Godley to form a band called Hotlegs ('Neanderthal Man' reaching No. 2 in the UK Charts), which morphed into the hugely successful 10cc in 1972. In 1982 Eric was invited to work on McCartney's first solo album after Wings disbanded.

Played on: *Tug of War*, *Pipes of Peace*, *Give My Regards to Broad Street* and *Press to Play*.

Where is he now? Eric worked as co-writer and producer on *Press to Play* but was replaced following disagreements. Since 1990 he has been involved with the Alan Parsons Project and has added two more solo albums to two previous releases in the Eighties. He lived in France for many years but returned to the UK in 2014 and now lives (not far from Paul) in the southeast of England.

Dave Mattacks

Born: 13 March 1948

Place of birth: Edgware, London, England

Dave Mattacks

Musical background: A multi-instrumentalist best known as the drummer for the English folk-rock band Fairport Convention (on and off) for almost 30 years, and as a very successful session player. Originally a professional piano tuner before taking up the drums, Dave was particularly influenced by the Shadows' original drummer Tony Meehan and the UK/US jazz drummers Kenny Clare and Paul Motian.

Played on: *Tug of War*, *Pipes of Peace*, *Give My Regards to Broad Street*, *Flowers in the Dirt* and *Run Devil Run*.

Where is he now? As a session drummer Dave has recorded and sometimes toured with just about everyone – from George Harrison, Cat Stevens, Elton John, Richard Thompson, Nick Drake, Georgie Fame, Jethro Tull, Steeleye Span, XTC... *ad infinitum*. In 1998, he moved to the USA near Boston, where he continues to be much in demand as a session and tour musician, record producer and member of the local band Super Genius.

Sir Richard Starkey

Ringo

Born: 7 July 1940

Place of birth: Liverpool, England

Musical background: Little point in introducing Sir Richard Starkey, better known as Ringo Starr, drummer for the Beatles from 1962 to 1970. A great lover of American country and western music, Ringo has cited his main influences as Hank Williams, Buck Owens, Willie Nelson, Johnny Cash, Kitty Wells, Hank Snow and the blues musician Lightnin' Hopkins. Far more impressed by c/w and blues performers rather than drummers per se, nevertheless he has mentioned US jazz drummers Chico Hamilton and Cozy Cole as being highly influential.

Played on: *Tug of War*, *Pipes of Peace*, *Give My Regards to Broad Street* and *Flaming Pie*.

Where is he now? Now 83 years of age, Ringo continues to record and returned to touring with his All-Starr Band in May 2022, but many gigs had to be cancelled or rescheduled when he and various band members tested positive for Covid-19. He has been inducted into the Rock & Roll Hall of Fame twice, as one of the Beatles and as a solo performer, and was knighted by Prince William in 2018. He's married to American actress and model Barbara Bach and has homes in Los Angeles, London and Monte Carlo.

James McCartney

Born: 12 September 1977

Place of birth: St John's Wood, London, England

Musical background: James spent almost the first three years of his life on tour with Wings, and several times during his teenage years, so not a bad education in

Biographies   117

James McCartney

a number of ways. He has said that his main influence on guitar is not his dad but Michael J. Fox's energy-popping solo on a cover of 'Johnny B. Goode' in the film *Back to the Future* (although Fox didn't actually play it). No doubt Paul provided one or two other useful tips as well.

Played on: *Press to Play*, *Flaming Pie* and *Driving Rain*.

Where is he now? James continues to concentrate on a solo career and spends most of his time in London.

Robbie McIntosh

Born: 25 October 1957

Place of birth: Sutton, Surrey, England

Musical background: Took up guitar at the age of 10, influenced by his two older sisters' record collections and his parents' love of music – his mother a piano player and father a jazz enthusiast. At 13, he started taking classical guitar lessons and developed deep admiration for Lightnin' Hopkins, the major factor in his love of blues music. Robbie played with various local bands from his teenage years with increasing success, eventually being invited to join the Pretenders in 1982 – a role he held for five years. He joined McCartney's band in 1988.

Played on: *Flowers in the Dirt* and *Off the Ground*. Also played on the live LPs *Tripping the Live Fantastic*, *Unplugged (The Official Bootleg)* and *Paul is Live*.

Where is he now? Robbie performed in Paul's band until 1993 when he resumed work as a session guitarist before forming his own band in 1998, which still performs regularly. As well as recording several solo albums, his career history as one of the world's most sought after session players is prodigious: Bee Gees, Rod Stewart, Celine Dion, Tom Jones, Barry Manilow, Joe Cocker, Roger Daltrey, Tori Amos, John Mayer, Norah Jones... Robbie lives in Weymouth, Dorset, on the south coast of England.

Robbie McIntosh

Hamish Stuart

Born: 8 October 1949

Place of birth: Glasgow, Scotland

Musical background: Hamish was influenced by his parents, who both sang in their local church choir, but also developed a love of soul music, particularly Mahalia Jackson. He formed his first band, the Dream Police, after leaving school and went on to join the Average White Band in 1972, recording 11 albums. He also performed with Chaka Khan from 1978 to '84 and joined Paul McCartney's band as guitarist/bass player, alongside Robbie McIntosh, in 1988.

Played on: *Flowers in the Dirt* and *Off the Ground*. Also played on the live LPs *Tripping the Live Fantastic*, *Unplugged (The Official Bootleg)* and *Paul is Live*.

Hamish Stuart

Where is he now? After leaving McCartney's band in 1993 Hamish worked as a session player and producer for several artists, recorded his first solo album and formed the Hamish Stuart Band. In 2006 he joined Ringo Starr and His All-Starr Band as touring bass player; he has recorded three live albums with the band and continues to perform with them. In 2015 he formed the 360 Band with two ex-Average White Band members. He lives near Faversham, Kent, where he runs the Three Mariners pub, known for good food and regular music events.

Paul 'Wix' Wickens

Born: 27 March 1956

Place of birth: Brentwood, Essex, England

Musical background: Paul was initially inspired by his parents, both musicians and lovers of classical and church music, who encouraged his music education from the age of about six. Paul attended Brentwood School and became friends with other pupils (one being Douglas Adams, author of *Hitchhiker's Guide to the Galaxy*) who introduced him to blues music, especially American pianist Pinetop Perkins. Other influences include Count Basie, Bill Payne (Little Feat) and Terry Adams (NRBQ – the New Rhythm and Blues Quintet). Paul is a multi-instrumentalist and in his early career performed with such leading artists as Kevin Coyne, Nik Kershaw, Paul Carrack, the Pretenders, Status Quo, Dave Gilmour, Was (Not Was) and Edie Brickell and the Bohemians before joining McCartney's band in 1989.

Played on: *Flowers in the Dirt*, *Off the Ground*, *Memory Almost Full*, *New* and *Egypt Station*. Also played on the live LPs *Tripping the Live Fantastic*, *Unplugged (The Official Bootleg)*, *Paul is Live*, *Back in the US Live 2002/Back in the World Live* and *Good Evening New York City*.

Biographies 119

Paul 'Wix' Wickens

up percussion at school in Wales at the age of 11. He played with the Welsh National Youth Orchestra and attended the Leeds College of Music at 16 to study classical music and jazz, but left a year early to concentrate on live work. Moved to London to take up session work and played with various bands including the Waterboys, Julian Cope and (with Paul Wickens) Edie Brickell and the Bohemians. Auditioned successfully for McCartney's band in 1987.

Played on: *Choba B CCCP* and *Flowers in the Dirt*. Also performed on the live LP *Tripping the Live Fantastic*.

Where is he now? Toured and recorded with McCartney for two years but left in 1991 to join Dire Straits' final two-year world tour. Has since become well-known for his work in electronic percussion and drum sampling. Lives in London.

Where is he now? 'Wix' is now Paul McCartney's longest serving musician, having taken over as the band's musical director more than 30 years ago and continuing to tour as their keyboard player, back-up guitarist and vocalist. He lives and runs his own small recording studio in north London.

Chris Whitten

Born: 26 March 1959

Place of birth: Wimbledon, southwest London, England

Musical background: Chris was inspired by his mother and older brother who introduced him as a young boy to the likes of the Beatles, Cream and Pink Floyd. Fascinated by the drums, he would bang along to their records on pots and pans before taking

Chris Whitten

Blair Cunningham

Born: 11 October 1957

Place of birth: Memphis, Tennessee, USA

Musical background: An American session drummer who has played with a wide range of international stars, from Mick Jagger and Roxy Music through to the Pretenders, Alison Moyet, Sade, Tina Turner and Lionel Richie. The youngest of 13 children, his oldest brother Kelly Cunningham Jr. taught all of his nine brothers to play drums.

Played on: *Off the Ground*. Also performed on live LPs *Unplugged (The Official Bootleg)* and *Paul is Live*.

Where is he now? Blair has lived in London since the late 1970s where he continues to work as a professional session drummer.

Blair Cunningham

Martin Glover

Martin Glover (Youth)

Born: 27 December 1960

Place of birth: Slough, Berkshire, England

Musical background: Martin is a founder member and bass player of the rock band Killing Joke, but perhaps better known as Youth, a record producer who, with Paul McCartney, created the experimental duo, the Fireman. A longtime exponent of electronic, ambient and dub music, Youth was hired to help with production on Paul's *Off the Ground* LP in 1992. Working well together, they collaborated on some new, more esoteric material, which evolved into their first album.

Played on: *Strawberries Oceans Ships Forest*, *Rushes*, *Liverpool Sound Collage* and *Electric Arguments*.

Where is he now? His record label, Butterfly Recordings, has handled production for a wide range of artists releases, from Take That and Tom Jones to electronic dance bands such as the Orb and System 7. He lives in southwest London.

Mick Green

Born: 22 February 1944

Place of birth: Matlock, Derbyshire, England

Musical background: Mick grew up in a block of flats in Wimbledon, southwest London, alongside future members of the band, the Pirates. A big fan of skiffle music and rock 'n' roll, he played in a skiffle trio called the Wayfaring Strangers at the age of 12 and came second in a competition to the Quarrymen – the early Beatles. In 1962 the trio all joined Johnny Kidd and the Pirates. Kidd died in 1966 but the Pirates reformed in 1976 and became one of the hardest-working and best-loved bands in the UK, releasing four successful LPs. A big admirer of Mick's guitar playing, McCartney employed him specifically in 1987 and 1999 for the raw sound he wanted on his two rock 'n' roll covers albums.

Played on: *Choba B CCCP* and *Run Devil Run*.

Where is he now? From 1999 to 2008, Mick performed regularly with Van Morrison live and in the studio but, in February 2004, while on tour with Bryan Ferry in New Zealand, he suffered a cardiac arrest on stage. Doctors in the audience saved his life and, on returning to the UK, he recovered sufficiently to carry on performing. Sadly, his health deteriorated once again in 2009 and, in January 2010, he died aged 65 of heart failure while in hospital in Ilford, Essex.

Mick Green

Rusty Anderson

Born: 20 January 1959

Place of birth: La Habra, California, USA

Musical background: Rusty took up guitar at a very early age and turned professional at just 14 in the Los Angeles band Eulogy. He had a successful solo career for 20 years before joining the rock band Ednaswap in 1993, recording four albums over five years. In 2001 he and drummer Abe Laboriel Jr. were invited by record producer David Kahne to perform on the recording of McCartney's album *Driving Rain*.

Played on: *Driving Rain*, *Chaos and Creation in the Backyard*, *Memory Almost Full*, *New*, *Egypt Station* and *McCartney III*. Also played on the live LPs *Back in the US Live 2002/Back in the World Live*, *Good Evening New York City* and *Amoeba Gig*.

Rusty Anderson

Where is he now? Still performing with McCartney as recently as 2022 at the conclusion of the 'Got Back Tour', taking in 16 US shows plus a warm-up gig in Frome, Somerset, followed the next night by topping the bill at nearby Glastonbury Festival. Rusty continues to work as a session musician, songwriter and producer and has also recorded four solo albums. He still spends most of his time in his hometown, La Habra, southeast of Los Angeles.

Abe Laboriel Jr.

Born: 23 March 1971

Place of birth: Boston, USA

Musical background: The son of the Mexican jazz bass player Abraham Laboriel Sr. (and his mother, a classically trained singer), Abe took up drums at the age of just four years old. Through his father's contacts he was tutored by the likes of Jeff Porcaro (Toto) and Alex Acuña, the drummer in his father's band, Koinonia. Also studied at two schools of music in Los Angeles and the Berklee College of Music in Boston. Has toured with the likes of Steve Vai, Seal, k.d. lang and Sting. Along with Rusty Anderson, Abe was invited by producer David Kahne to join Paul's band for the recording of the album *Driving Rain*.

Played on: *Driving Rain, Chaos and Creation in the Backyard, Memory Almost Full, New, Egypt Station* and *McCartney III*. Also played on the live LPs *Back in the US Live 2002/Back in the World Live, Good Evening New York City* and *Amoeba Gig*.

Where is he now? Still performing with McCartney as recently as Glastonbury 2022 on the 'Got Back Tour'. Has worked as a session drummer but also plays guitar, bass, keyboards and sings vocals in various music projects including his own one-man band, Sprinkle. Lives in Los Angeles.

Abe Laboriel Jr.

Brian Ray

Born: 4 January 1955

Place of birth: Southern California, USA

Musical background: A session guitar/bass player, Brian took up the instrument at the age of nine encouraged and prominently inspired by his sister Jean, 15 years older and a member of the respected folk duo Jim and Jean. Other major influences were Ray Davies, Randy Newman, Tom Petty and Bob Dylan. As a teenager, Brian's professional career got underway as guitarist for Bobby Pickett, through which he became the guitarist (and eventually music director) for Etta James for (on and off) over 20 years. He was introduced to McCartney by drummer Abe Laboriel Jr. and joined the band for the 'Driving Rain Tour' in 2002.

Played on: *Chaos and Creation in the Backyard*, *Memory Almost Full*, *New* and *Egypt Station*. Also played on the live LPs *Back in the US Live 2002/Back in the World Live*, *Good Evening New York City* and *Amoeba Gig*.

Brian Ray

Where is he now? Still performing with McCartney as recently as Glastonbury Festival 2022 on the 'Got Back Tour'. Brian also runs his own record label in Los Angeles, Whooray Records, for which he has recorded two solo albums. He lives west of Los Angeles in the coastal city of Santa Monica.

Rusty, Abe, Paul and Brian perform on stage at The SSE Hydro in Glasgow, December 14, 2018

Discography
Studio Albums

McCartney

Released: 17 April 1970
Label: Apple
Producer: Paul McCartney
Recorded: McCartney's home in Cavendish Avenue, Morgan Studios, and Abbey Road Studios, London
UK: No. 2
USA: No. 1

Side 1:
1. The Lovely Linda
2. That Would Be Something
3. Valentine Day
4. Every Night
5. Hot as Sun/Glasses
6. Junk
7. Man We Was Lonely

Side 2:
1. Oo You
2. Momma Miss America
3. Teddy Boy
4. Singalong Junk
5. Maybe I'm Amazed
6. Kreen-Akrore

Following the chaos at Apple and Paul's period of depression hidden away up in Scotland, McCartney returned to London just before Christmas 1969 and began working on his first solo album at home in Cavendish Avenue. Playing all of the instruments himself, with Linda contributing backing vocals, everything was recorded onto a recently purchased four-track tape machine. The set-up was about as basic as it gets, especially for a member of the world's biggest band.

The first song recorded on tape was a brief fragment of an unfinished song he'd been writing in Scotland, 'The Lovely Linda'; it was intended only to be used to try out the new equipment, but it finished up as the opening track. The second number 'That Would Be Something' was also written in Scotland, while the instrumental 'Valentine Day' was made up as he went along, as was another instrumental 'Momma Miss America' on Side 2.

* Please note: all songs written by Paul McCartney unless stated otherwise.

It was these instrumentals (four out of 13 tracks in total) that left many Beatles fans disappointed with this album, and it's easy to understand why. Of the four, only 'Hot as Sun/Glasses' with its Latin rhythms could be described as a pleasant listen (despite ending with 35 seconds of water-filled wine glasses being rubbed to make them ring); and while the two numbers already mentioned are acceptable, the final track 'Kreen-Akrore' (a drum solo based on an Amazonian tribe's rhythmic percussion he'd seen on a TV documentary), is not something you'd want to include on a chill-out album.

It's a shame, because it's these numbers from *McCartney* that tend to get mentioned rather than the mesmerising 'Junk' and 'Teddy Boy' (both written in India in 1968); the sublime 'Every Night' and 'Maybe I'm Amazed' (both written and played during the Beatles' *Get Back!* sessions); and the jaunty 'Man We Was Lonely', written just before the album was completed to convey how they were coping ok, despite the Beatles' split. With two or three stronger numbers in preference to rather weak instrumentals, the result could have been a solo masterpiece. To be fair, he was in a big hurry, desperate to get something out there, but what might have been created if this had been delayed and *Ram* had evolved into a double solo album a year later?

Instead, we're left with a decent 'love or hate' album that some will never be persuaded is worth taking too seriously. On the day it was released *McCartney* gathered stinging criticism for being under-produced, unfinished (only 34 minutes long) and unlistenable; music journalists queued up to get their punches in: "sheer banality" (*Melody Maker*); "distinctly second-rate" (*Rolling Stone*); "no substance... he seems to believe that anything that comes into his head is worth having. And he's wrong..." (*Guardian*).

Some loved it, of course, and nowadays more people are warming to *McCartney*, maybe even recognising some truth in Paul's self-analysis in *Rolling Stone* magazine that this was rock's first indie album. It's a valid point; overall this was an impressive piece of work with several numbers that could easily have appeared on *Abbey Road* or *Let it Be*. Not bad for something created in a few weeks in his living room.

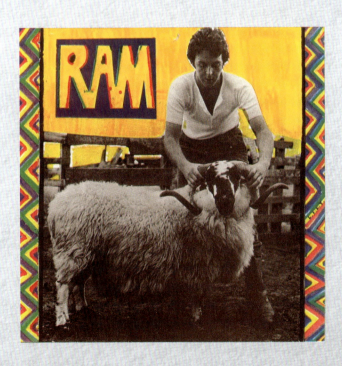

RAM
(Paul and Linda McCartney)

Released:	17 May 1971
Label:	Apple
Producer:	Paul and Linda McCartney
Recorded:	CBS Studios, and A&R Studios, New York; Sound Recorders Studio, Hollywood, Los Angeles
UK:	No. 1
USA:	No. 2

Side 1:

1. **Too Many People**
2. **3 Legs**
3. **Ram On**
4. **Dear Boy** (Paul/Linda McCartney)
5. **Uncle Albert/Admiral Halsey** (Paul/Linda McCartney)
6. **Smile Away**

Side 2:

1. **Heart of the Country** (Paul/Linda McCartney)
2. **Monkberry Moon Delight** (Paul/Linda McCartney)
3. **Eat at Home** (Paul/Linda McCartney)
4. **Long Haired Lady** (Paul/Linda McCartney)
5. **Ram On**
6. **The Back Seat of My Car**

Six months after a disappointing response to McCartney's first solo album, and amid the legal disagreements taking place in the High Court to bring the Beatles' partnership to an end, Paul and Linda headed over to New York to begin work on *Ram*. In an attempt to deal with much of the criticism aimed at *McCartney* regarding its low-fi, one-man band approach, they recruited guitarists David Spinozza and Hugh McCracken, and future Wings drummer Denny Seiwell, before getting underway at New York's CBS Studios (aka Columbia Studios).

Despite their best efforts, it was inevitable (given the fall-out between Paul and his former bandmates) that they would not be nominating *Ram* for album of the year. John Lennon hated it and claimed that some lyrics were aimed at him and Yoko (which they were), particularly "Too many people preaching practices" and "You took your lucky break and broke it in two." Harrison was no less unimpressed and even Ringo commented: "I feel sad about Paul's albums... I don't think there's one tune on the last one, *Ram*." It must have been painful to McCartney that such criticism was coming from one of his closest friends, especially as it was a ridiculous thing to say. It's an unusual album, that's true, but rammed full of good songs – so many that Paul found it difficult to decide which of the 20-plus numbers recorded during the session should be included. Eventually that was left to sound engineer Eirik Wangberg at Sound Recorders in Los Angeles who was given free rein to mix the songs as he thought best. The result was a wonderful mish-mash of material, any of which would have

sat comfortably on the 'White Album', and some equally on *Abbey Road*. Best of them all is possibly 'Uncle Albert/Admiral Halsey' – a comedic combination of unfinished songs mashed together by Wangberg in the studio – one a portrayal of a heavy-drinking relative, the other concerning a genuine US Admiral during WWII, and a third brief section encouraging a gypsy lifestyle. All in all, bonkers, but brilliant.

'3 Legs', another veiled dig at Paul's former bandmates (*"Well I thought you was my friend, but you let me down, put my heart around the bend"*), is followed by 'Ram On', a nice ballad played on a ukulele celebrating a simple lifestyle, and 'Dear Boy', said to be about Linda's first husband Mel See concerning his lack of appreciation towards her – both songs offering beautiful baroque, Beach Boys-style, backing vocal harmonies. The vocals from Paul and Linda throughout the entire album are superb. While it's true that the second side doesn't quite maintain that same high standard throughout, it's still pretty good, offering 'The Back Seat of My Car' as the grand finale with orchestration added by the New York Philharmonic (as on 'Long Haired Lady' and 'Uncle Albert/Admiral Halsey').

While criticism from former bandmates had been hard to accept, it was less surprising to discover serious journalists weren't big fans either: "incredibly inconsequential" and "monumentally irrelevant" said *Rolling Stone* , while *NME* accused *Ram* of possessing "not one worthwhile or lasting piece of music" before concluding: "*Ram* is the worst thing Paul McCartney has ever done".

Where did such floods of poisoned ink come from? And why? It was typical of the level of critical abuse McCartney would have to tolerate until *Band on the Run* arrived, and for long periods after that. Decades after *Ram*'s release, critics have reviewed the album more favourably with some (and many fans) describing it as one of McCartney's best ever solo albums; even *Rolling Stone* was decent enough to eat stale humble pie and describe *Ram* very accurately as a "daffy masterpiece" and "a grand psychedelic ramble full of divine melodies and orchestral frippery". The very things for which McCartney had been attacked in print were now regarded as evidence of his genius. A bit like Mozart, really. How opinions can change over 50 years or more. *Ram* is, and always has been, a wonderful piece of music.

RAM ON:
The 50th anniversary tribute to Paul & Linda McCartney's RAM

Released in 2021 by Spirit of Unicorn Music, *Ram On* is a re-imagining (with Paul's approval) of the now much-loved *Ram*, with the involvement of three of the musicians who appeared on the LP back in 1971 – original guitarist David Spinozza and flugelhorn player Marvin Stamm (on 'Uncle Albert/Admiral Halsey') are joined by drummer Denny Seiwell (as co-producer with multi-instrumentalist Fernando Perdomo) – plus over 100 talented, younger musicians from around the world. The album also includes new versions from the *Ram* sessions of the superb single 'Another Day' c/w 'Oh Woman Oh Why'.

Wild Life
Wings

Released: 7 December 1971
Label: Apple
Producer: Paul McCartney
Recorded: Abbey Road Studios, London
UK: No. 11
USA: No. 10

All songs written by Paul and Linda McCartney unless stated otherwise.

Side 1:
1. **Mumbo**
2. **Bip Bop**
3. **Love is Strange** (Ethel Smith)
4. **Wild Life**

Side 2:
1. **Some People Never Know**
2. **I Am Your Singer**
3. **Bip Bop (Link)**
4. **Tomorrow**
5. **Dear Friend**
6. **Mumbo (Link)**

The newly formed Wings laid down their first album in just eight days in an attempt to capture the rawness of a live studio recording. Always seems a good idea at the time, but so often proves otherwise. This album just about scrapes through as a success, although many disagree. Five of the eight songs were recorded in just one take at Abbey Road Studios after a short period of rehearsals at the McCartney's home studio in Scotland. 'Mumbo', for example, was little more than a loose jam recorded by the sound engineer, but Paul liked it enough to hang on to it. The album also included a tongue-in-cheek reggae remake of Mickey & Sylvia's 1957 hit 'Love Is Strange'.

The Side 1 closing title track and Side 2 opener 'Some People Never Know' are both good numbers and there's nothing on this album that sounds out of place, but only one standout track: the closing 'Dear Friend' (apart from the short 'Mumbo Link'). Recorded during the *Ram* sessions - an attempt to smooth over personal problems with Lennon after John's bitter lyrics on *Imagine*'s 'How Do You Sleep?' – the song at least indicated Paul's intentions to try to repair their relationship. The song certainly wouldn't have been out of place on *Abbey Road* or, more appropriately, on one of his first two solo albums.

Overall *Wild Life* was considered second-rate by many music pundits. Roy Hollingworth from *Melody Maker* described it as "a discotheque album ... too many maracas around and not enough balls". Others were far more critical without any real justification. For Wings' first LP knocked out in a matter of weeks, it's not bad at all.

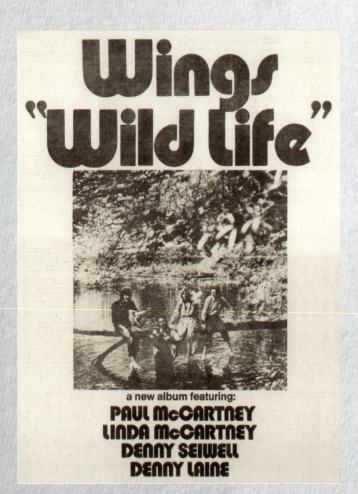

Red Rose Speedway
Wings

Released:	30 April 1973
Label:	Apple
Producer:	Paul McCartney
Recorded:	Abbey Road Studios, Olympic Sound, Morgan Studios, Trident Studios, and Island Studios, London; CBS Studios, New York; Sound Recorders Studio, Hollywood, Los Angeles
UK:	No. 5
USA:	No. 1

All songs written by Paul and Linda McCartney

Side 1:
1. Big Barn Bed
2. My Love
3. Get on the Right Thing
4. One More Kiss
5. Little Lamb Dragonfly

Side 2:
1. Single Pigeon
2. When the Night
3. Loup (1st Indian On the Moon)
4. Medley:
Hold Me Tight | Lazy Dynamite | Hands of Love | Power Cut

Wings' second studio album was credited to Paul McCartney and Wings in an effort to improve the public's familiarity of the band, following disappointing sales for *Wild Life*. Something worked because this album became a Top 5 hit, but was that because it was much better? It certainly could have been.

Originally planned as a double LP (see below), it was reduced down to a single album by EMI who didn't consider some of the material good enough. Whether or not they kept the best songs for the single LP is debatable – band members Denny Laine and new guitarist Henry McCullough both later expressed opinions that the double album would have been, and the single album could have been, a lot more impressive.

Laine was particularly unhappy when two of his songs were dropped, while McCullough felt that several of McCartney's rockier tracks should have been retained, rather than the lighter material selected. Linda agreed: "Something was missing," she said, in an interview with *Sounds* magazine. "We needed a heavier sound. It was a terribly unsure period." The original producer Glyn Johns expressed similar feelings about the band and songs. After a month he quit the project altogether.

Was it that bad? No, most definitely not. Side 1 is terrific – five great songs that never waver or diminish – particularly McCartney's 'My Love' with the inspired guitar solo played by McCullough off the top of his head. True, Side 2 is not of the same calibre throughout, but the opening two tracks are also very good; 'Loup' and a Beatles-style medley to conclude the album... not so good.

EMI's fears that *Red Rose Speedway* would be a dismal failure proved an unnecessary overreaction. It's a decent album that showed positive progress as a follow-up to the band's debut. Without EMI's interference, if left as a double album, it would have been better still.

Red Rose Speedway:
ORIGINAL DOUBLE ALBUM

In 2018, MPL Communications reconstructed and released for the first time the original planned *Red Rose Speedway* double album. It was not clear as to what the original running order was until it was discovered that drummer Denny Seiwell still had three of the four acetates of the double album, dated 13 December 1972, and a written tracklisting for the fourth side. McCartney's archive department later found a revised tracklisting from 30 January 1973 and, as the album was released on 30 April 1973, it was agreed that must be the more accurate version. The double album has been newly remastered at Abbey Road Studios.

Tracklisting with additional songs highlighted in purple.
All songs written by Paul and Linda McCartney unless stated otherwise.

Side 1:

1. Night Out
2. Get on the Right Thing
3. Country Dreamer (*B-side to Helen Wheels*)
4. Big Barn Bed
5. My Love

Side 2:

1. Single Pigeon
2. When the Night
3. Seaside Woman (Linda McCartney) (*single released under the name Suzy and the Red Stripes*)
4. I Lie Around (*B-side to Live and Let Die*)
5. The Mess (*live at the Hague, Netherlands*)

Side 3:

1. Best Friend (*live in Antwerp, Belgium*)
2. Loup (1st Indian On the Moon)
3. Medley:
Hold Me Tight | Lazy Dynamite | Hands of Love | Power Cut

Side 4:

1. Mama's Little Girl (*B-side to Put it There*)
2. I Would Only Smile (Denny Laine)
3. One More Kiss
4. Tragedy (Gerald H. Nelson and Fred B. Burch)
5. Little Lamb Dragonfly

Discography 131

Band On The Run
Wings

Released: 5 December 1973
Label: Apple
Producer: Paul McCartney
Recorded: EMI Studios, and ARC Studios, Lagos, Nigeria; Associated Independent Recording (AIR) Studios, Abbey Road Studios, and Kingsway Recorders, London
UK: No. 1
USA: No. 1

All songs written by Paul and Linda McCartney unless stated otherwise.

Side 1:
1. **Band On the Run**
2. **Jet**
3. **Bluebird**
4. **Mrs Vandebilt**
5. **Let Me Roll It**

Side 2:
1. **Mamunia**
2. **No Words** (Paul McCartney/Denny Laine)
3. **Picasso's Last Words (Drink to Me)**
4. **Nineteen Hundred and Eighty Five**

Here, ladies and gentlemen, is the Wings equivalent to Fleetwood Mac's *Rumours*; a nigh-on perfect record, created out of adversity; an album that should be celebrated, applauded, enjoyed and recognised as something that will never be equalled: *Band on the Run*. Paul loved it, the public loved it, the media loved it, even John Lennon loved it! At last, Paul McCartney had been handed the plaudits he desired (and deserved) but had been denied since, according to many, he broke up the Beatles.

For McCartney, this was his chance to prove what he was still capable of and escape from the media entrapment that appeared to have written him off as a composer of melodic ditties and 'granny music'. This was the album that fans and critics had been waiting for: his best post-Beatles release and certainly the most impressive from Wings; a succession of terrific songs full of emotion, romance, originality, humour, diversity, pace and energy verging on a par with the 'White Album'. From the delightful, folky three-part opening title song all the way through to the throbbing 'Nineteen Hundred and Eighty Five' rocker, there's not one weak or predictable number on this LP that should have been jettisoned. And what's remarkable is that this album was produced during one of Paul and his band's most troubled

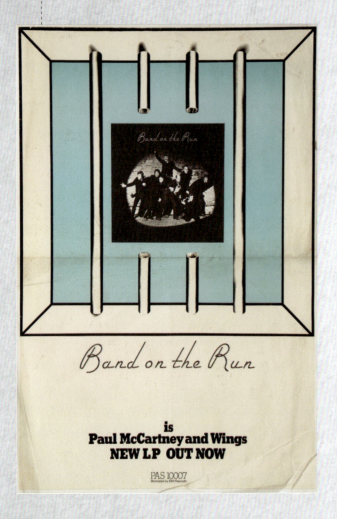

hours before their flight was due to depart, drummer Denny Seiwell rang to tell them he wasn't going either. Only Paul, Linda, Denny Laine, the Beatles' former sound engineer, Geoff Emerick and two roadies would be making the trip. With McCartney having to take care of lead vocals, drums, bass, some keyboards and most of the lead guitar parts, he and what was left of Wings worked their way through a succession of terrific numbers, most of which had been written and rehearsed at their High Park Farm in Scotland. Would the album have been even better if McCullough and Seiwell hadn't jumped ship at the last minute? Probably not. McCartney had the bit between his teeth and there was no way, despite everything, this album could not succeed.

'Band on the Run', alongside several other songs on the album, reflected basic themes of 'escape' and 'freedom' with the opening line "*Stuck inside these four walls, sent inside forever*" expressing Paul's anger at getting busted for possession of pot and determination to break out of a music industry that seemed no longer to believe in him – hence the album cover depicting the band surrounded by six well-known celebrities dressed as convicts caught up against the wall in a prison searchlight.

'Jet', the first song released as a single, was named after the McCartney's black Labrador puppy, according to Paul (although he did on another occasion claim it was actually about one of their black ponies!); it must have been a pretty crazy dog (or pony) if the lyrics are anything to go by. Nobody understands what it's all about, but it's a wonderful pop song. (Paul and wife Nancy adopted a puppy from a Los Angeles rescue centre in July 2023 - renamed Jet.)

'Bluebird' is understandably often compared to 'Blackbird' from the Beatles' 'White Album'; another acoustic love ballad, with lovely vocal harmonies from Linda and Denny, the song celebrates two lovebirds that fly away together to find freedom. Session player Howie Casey adds a superb saxophone solo as the icing on the cake.

times. If Fleetwood Mac had to record *Rumours* while dealing with divorce and affairs, Wings had to cope with near-death experiences!

Paul and Linda McCartney knew this album had to be good or their music career would be under fire once again, so they decided to record somewhere more adventurous than the UK; from EMI's extensive list of international studios, they chose Lagos in Nigeria in the belief that, in August, it would be warm and sunny, in an effort to inspire them to come up with something new. Just a week before they were due to depart, however, their best laid plans began to fall apart.

First, guitarist Henry McCullough quit the band following a disagreement with McCartney, combined with his complete lack of belief in Linda's musical ability. A week later, just a few

The boisterous 'Mrs Vandebilt' continues the 'freedom' theme with Paul paraphrasing an old humorous rhyme used by the English comedian Charlie Chester as a way to celebrate low-cost living: "*Down in the jungle, living in a tent, better than a prefab, no rent*". After the fun element comes the angst of one of the highlights of the album, the slow blues rock number 'Let Me Roll It'. According to McCartney the song was actually about rolling a joint, rather than a John Lennon pastiche using tape echo and short stabs of guitar, which many critics thought was the case. Either way, it's brilliant.

The title of 'Mamunia' was taken from an expensive hotel in Marrakesh called 'Mamounia' where they had stayed on holiday the year before. With its close vocal harmonies once again, there's almost certainly an element of Crosby, Stills and Nash in this one – no surprise given their popular song 'Marrakesh Express'.

'No Words' is the only track on the album to be co-written with Denny Laine and another excellent mid-tempo love song to which has been added some lush string quartet orchestration by the arranger Tony Visconti. The same applies to 'Picasso's Last Words (Drink to Me)' – McCartney's response to a challenge from the actor Dustin Hoffman who they visited in Jamaica during the filming of *Papillon*. Tossing over a copy of a magazine including an article on the artist Picasso's death, and saying write a song about that, McCartney picked up his guitar and wrote it in a matter of minutes. Witnessing McCartney's songwriting skills being displayed in droves, Hoffman was dumfounded.

As the album's magnificent sign-off number comes 'Nineteen Hundred and Eighty Five', a hard rocker about not much at all but based on a simple rhyme hanging around in Paul's brainbox for months: "*No one ever left alive in nineteen hundred and eighty-five*." With its 'Lady Madonna'-like piano intro, heavy drumming and guitar, slow middle-eight interludes before a climactic finale, again featuring Tony

Visconti's dramatic string arrangement, and finally, in Beatles style, a short reprise of 'Band on the Run'. Job done.

Returning to London in September after seven weeks in Lagos, the tapes were copied onto a 16-track machine for overdubbing at George Martin's AIR Studios; on the first listen it was clear they had something special. Once 'Nineteen Hundred and Eighty Five' had been recorded, overdubs added and the cover artwork complete, it was time to put it to the test. Thankfully, when released in December '73, almost everyone agreed, for once, it was a brilliant piece of work.

Even two publications responsible for some of the most vitriolic reviews over the last three years admitted defeat: Said *NME*: 'The ex-Beatle least likely to re-establish his credibility and lead the field has pulled it off with a positive master-stroke of an album..." While Jon Landau of *Rolling Stone* described the album as "with the possible exception of John Lennon's *Plastic Ono Band*, the finest record yet released by any of the four musicians who were once called the Beatles".

In later years, given time to mature and gain appreciation from a wider, younger audience, Q magazine elevated *Band on the Run* to No. 75 in its 2000 list of the '100 Greatest British Albums Ever'; in 2012 it was listed at No. 418 on *Rolling Stone* magazine's revised list of 'the 500 Greatest Albums of All Time'. There are many other examples of such high praise and recognition.

Perhaps more importantly to Paul, the album has gone on to sell almost 9 million copies worldwide. As *Melody Maker* put it: "The feeling expressed throughout is one of happy, almost exultant freedom..."

Wings were on the run at last.

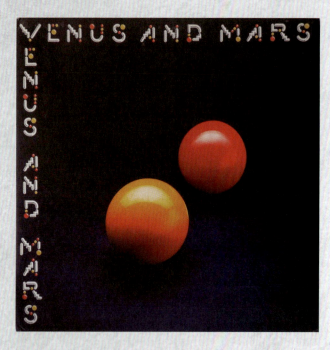

Venus and Mars
Wings

Released:	27 May 1975
Label:	Capitol
Producer:	Paul McCartney
Recorded:	Abbey Road Studios, London; Sea-Saint Recording Studio, New Orleans; Wally Heider Studios, Los Angeles
UK:	No. 1
USA:	No. 1

All songs written by Paul and Linda McCartney unless stated otherwise.

Side 1:
1. **Venus and Mars**
2. **Rock Show**
3. **Love in Song**
4. **You Gave Me the Answer**
5. **Magneto and Titanium Man**
6. **Letting Go**

Side 2:
1. **Venus and Mars - Reprise**
2. **Spirits Of Ancient Egypt**
3. **Medicine Jar** (Jimmy McCulloch/Colin Allen)
4. **Call Me Back Again**
5. **Listen to What The Man Said**
6. **Treat Her Gently/Lonely Old People**
7. **Crossroads** (Tony Hatch)

After *Band on the Run*, McCartney was sensible enough not to attempt a Wings 'White Album' follow-up equivalent (especially as EMI had already displayed a complete lack of enthusiasm for doubles). Instead, Wings simply continued their run of commercial success with a straightforward rock album to launch their 'Wings Over the World Tour'.

As things had gone so well with previous recordings in Lagos, the decision was made, after laying down some basic tracks at Abbey Road, to head abroad once more, to the Sea-Saint Studios in New Orleans, with two new band members in tow – Scotsman Jimmy McCulloch on guitar and Englishman Geoff Britton on drums: a sometimes explosive combination. Personal tensions and differences between two very different characters resulted in Britton being sacked after just six months, having played on only three of the songs. An American session player, Joe English, was recruited to finish the album.

Even if the band members hadn't had much of a chance to make friends, the good news was that *Venus and Mars* was far more coherent and thematic than anything before *Band on the Run*. The opening title track served as a perfect overture to live shows before the band took to the stage each night, kicking off with the heavier than normal 'Rock Show'. Side 1 continues with a succession of excellent numbers demonstrating the breadth of McCartney's songwriting skills: a lovely ballad 'Love in Song' followed by a Forties crooner number 'You Gave Me the Answer', the rather bizarre 'Magneto and Titanium Man', and Beatles-esque 'Letting Go'.

Side 2 isn't far behind with the likes of McCulloch's 'Medicine Jar', written with Colin Allen (lyricist and former drummer of the Glaswegian band Stone the Crows), the terrific single 'Listen to What the Man Said' and even the concluding medley of 'Treat Her Gently/ Lonely Old People' drawing the album to a satisfying conclusion before the soppy version of the *Crossroads* TV show's theme tune, cueing gagging noises from various music pundits across the UK. It actually works quite well, in truth, despite what the likes of *NME* thought at the time: "…set the Blandometer to 'Prawn Cocktail' and away we go."

Easy listening, in other words. As Paul would question on the next Wings album: "What's wrong with that?"

Wings At The Speed Of Sound
Wings

Released:	25 March 1976
Label:	Capitol
Producer:	Paul McCartney
Recorded:	Abbey Road Studios, London
UK:	No. 2
USA:	No. 1

All songs written by Paul and Linda McCartney unless stated otherwise.

Side 1:
1. Let 'Em In
2. The Note You Never Wrote
3. She's My Baby
4. Beware My Love
5. Wino Junko (Jimmy McCulloch/Colin Allen)

Side 2:
1. Silly Love Songs
2. Cook of the House
3. Time to Hide (Denny Laine)
4. Must Do Something About It
5. San Ferry Anne
6. Warm and Beautiful

Wings at the Speed of Sound was recorded at Abbey Road, released and performed among the chaos of the band's highly successful 'Wings Over the World Tour'. This was the album that should have proved to at least some of those critics who claimed Wings were not a proper rock band (just McCartney's backing musicians), that there was real, in-depth talent here.

Every member of the band took over the lead vocals on at least one song, and Paul encouraged everyone to contribute a song during the sessions (as on *Red Rose Speedway*, much to EMI's chagrin); 'Wino Junko' was composed (and sung) by Jimmy McCulloch, co-written again with Colin Allen. Denny Laine's 'Time to Hide' was equally impressive, while drummer Joe English took over lead vocals on 'Must Do Something About It' very capably in his impressive, David Cassidy soundalike voice. Denny Laine's vocal interpretation of the McCartney's 'The Note You Never Wrote' is up there with the album's two big hits that open each side, 'Let 'Em In' and 'Silly Love Songs' – Paul's response to the critics who described much of his previous material as exactly that.

Despite the album's high standards, the critical kickings continued; a *Rolling Stone* reviewer described it as a "Day with the McCartneys" concept album, which few buyers would probably understand or agree with. Whatever, *Wings at the Speed of Sound* sold 3.5 million copies worldwide. Paul's response to the critics may well have been "stick that in your pipe and smoke it". Or something along those lines.

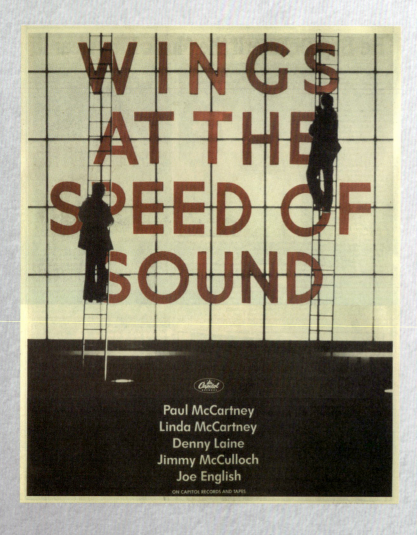

Discography 137

London Town
Wings

Released:	31 March 1978
Label:	Parlophone/Capitol
Producer:	Paul McCartney
Recorded:	Abbey Road Studios, and AIR Studios, London; Record Plant Mobile Studio, Watermelon Cay, Virgin Islands (aboard the yacht *Fair Carol*); Spirit of Ranachan Studio, Campbeltown, Scotland
UK:	No. 4
USA:	No. 2

Side 1:

1. **London Town** (Paul McCartney/Denny Laine)
2. **Cafe on the Left Bank**
3. **I'm Carrying**
4. **Backwards Traveller**
5. **Cuff Link**
6. **Children Children** (Paul McCartney/Denny Laine)
7. **Girlfriend**
8. **I've Had Enough**

Side 2:

1. **With a Little Luck**
2. **Famous Groupies**
3. **Deliver Your Children** (McCartney/Laine)
4. **Name and Address**
5. **Don't Let it Bring You Down** (McCartney/Laine)
6. **Morse Moose and the Grey Goose** (McCartney/Laine)

Work on the sixth Wings album *London Town* got underway at Abbey Road in February 1977 with plans to promote the album on another major tour across Europe and the USA, but Linda announced that she was pregnant (with their son James) so the tour plans had to be put on hold. Instead, thought Paul, let's not hang around here in cold old London Town, but head off to record the album aboard a luxury yacht docked on the Virgin Islands in the Caribbean Sea.

Reflecting the nautical setting, the album's working title was the rather amusing 'Water Wings' but recording on a boat, next to another boat where they ate and slept, proved not as simple (or glamorous) as anticipated. Accidents happened, people got sunburnt, equipment got damaged, everyone got frustrated and, as Linda's pregnancy neared its conclusion, the band halted the sessions and returned to London. At around the same time as Linda gave birth to James in September 1977, Joe English quit (suffering from US homesickness), while Jimmy McCulloch quit to join the Small Faces. Once again, for the second time, Wings had been reduced to a trio.

London Town became, in effect, Wings' folk album, with some great songs including the title track opener and two acoustic numbers, 'Deliver Your Children' and 'Don't Let it Bring You Down', both on the subject of staying positive co-written by McCartney and Denny Laine. Throughout, however, the album lacks consistency, energy or excitement and proves disjointed, just chugging along to a disappointingly merciful conclusion. The big question, of course, is why wasn't 'Mull of Kintyre', recorded in 1977, included on the album? Adding what became the biggest selling UK single of all time (and still in the Top 5) would have made a huge difference.

As one might expect, *London Town* received some noncommittal reviews from music critics and it seemed as if they (and fans) had run out of steam: couldn't be bothered to buy or even criticise it. Despite achieving Top 5 status in both the UK and USA, it lacked the same level of impetus and staying power of Wings' previous releases and sort of faded away into the mist of a London peasouper. Capitol, in Paul's opinion, simply hadn't promoted *London Town* anywhere near enough in the USA. Columbia would be Wings' next (and final) port of call.

Back To The Egg
Wings

Released:	8 June 1979
Label:	Parlophone/Capitol
Producer:	Paul McCartney and Chris Thomas
Recorded:	Spirit of Ranachan, Campbeltown, Scotland; Lympne Castle, Kent, England; Abbey Road Studios, and Replica Studio, London
UK:	No. 6
USA:	No. 8

Side 1:
1. Reception
2. Getting Closer
3. We're Open Tonight
4. Spin It Out
5. Again And Again And Again (Denny Laine)
6. Old Siam, Sir
7. Arrow Through Me

Side 2:
1. Rockestra Theme
2. To You
3. After the Ball/Million Miles
4. Winter Rose/Love Awake
5. The Broadcast
6. So Glad to See You Here
7. Baby's Request

Co-produced by Chris Thomas (who had worked on the Beatles' 'White Album' and gone on to be producer on the Sex Pistol's classic album *Never Mind the Bollocks*), Wings' final studio album reflected Paul's attempt to at least engage with new wave music, both in terms of the album's title (Linda's idea) and the loose theme of a raw rock 'n' roll band back on the road. With two new band members in tow – Laurence Juber on guitar and Steve Holley on drums – the album was originally conceived once again as a double and, despite the intention of some rough edges, it was almost a year before recording at four different studio locations was completed.

The album's opening instrumental 'Reception' finds McCartney trying to tune into a radio station before three rocky, somewhat punkier songs – 'Getting Closer' being the best – remain loyal to the loose concept of a band on the road. Laine's only number 'Again and Again and Again' follows on in similar vein. McCartney returns with two decent songs, 'Old Siam, Sir' and the funky soul-influenced 'Arrow Through Me'.

Side 2 introduces the rather dubious concept of the 'Rockestra Theme', a largely instrumental number performed by a who's who of old- and new-wave rockers from the likes of the Shadows and Led Zeppelin through to the Pretenders and the Attractions. (Pointless, maybe, but did win a Grammy as 'Best Rock Instrumental Performance' in 1980.) Side 2 glides through two gospel-influenced medleys 'After the Ball/Million Miles' and 'Winter Rose/Love Awake' before a 'Rockestra Theme' reprise and Forties-style crooner, 'Baby's Request', brings down the curtain to mild applause.

Although Top 10 status was achieved in both the UK and USA, *Back to the Egg*'s overall sales were disappointing. To rub salt into the wounds, the album received some shocking reviews: "The sorriest grab bag of dreck in recent memory," summed up *Rolling Stone*. In *Melody Maker*, even dependable old Ray Coleman wrote that McCartney "seems to be on a treadmill of banality... the band offers nothing inspiring... this pleasant album," he concluded, "gets Wings nowhere..."

He wasn't wrong.

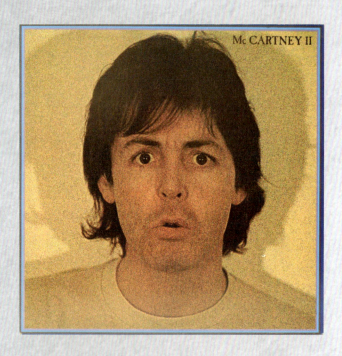

McCartney II

Released: 16 May 1980
Label: Parlophone/Capitol
Producer: Paul McCartney
Recorded: McCartney's home studio in Peasmarsh, East Sussex, England; Spirit of Ranachan, Campbeltown, Scotland; Abbey Road Studios, and Replica Studio, London
UK: No. 1
USA: No. 3

Side 1:
1. Coming Up
2. Temporary Secretary
3. On the Way
4. Waterfalls
5. Nobody Knows

Side 2:
1. Front Parlour
2. Summer's Day Song
3. Frozen Jap
4. Bogey Music
5. Darkroom
6. One of These Days

After the relative chaos of *Back to the Egg*, Paul spent the next three summer months of 1979 by himself in East Sussex and Scotland recording his second attempt at a genuine solo album, *McCartney II*. While he had dipped his toes into the new-wave pool with what became Wings' final LP, in an attempt to keep up with the new sounds now dominating the UK and US charts, this was diving in head first.

Once again envisioned as a double album, but thankfully persuaded once again to stick to just the one, Paul immediately reminded us what he was capable of with an opener as good as 'Coming Up', followed not far behind by 'Waterfalls' – one of those McCartney ballads to serve as a beacon for what he is renowned and loved for. The Alexis Korner inspired songs 'On the Way' and 'Nobody Knows', are decent blues numbers to round off Side 1. And Side 2's concluding number, 'One of These Days', is the sort of material most of us probably expected to enjoy on this new solo LP – low-tech recordings of heartbreaking, reflective, acoustic songs that guitar players across the world attempt to learn in their bedrooms.

What we certainly didn't expect is much of what surrounds that handful of decent songs on *McCartney II* – a crazy, electronic synth mess. 'Experimental' with a bit of Frank Zappa ('Temporary Secretary') thrown in is the best way to describe it.

One can only recognise and applaud McCartney's willingness and enthusiasm to embrace new concepts, new technology and new sounds... but not everyone wants to listen to it.

No surprise that some of the reviews for *McCartney II* were particularly cruel, even in *New Musical Express* – perhaps the one place, with its new wave leanings, one might have been less surprised if it had been hailed a new McCartney masterpiece. No chance. Commented *NME*'s Danny Baker: "*McCartney II* is not worth the plastic it's printed on. Neither is Paul..."

There are some who specialise in stupid, unnecessary comments but, as Paul has often discovered, sticking your head above the parapet can often result in bad outcomes. Taking risks has never been something that bothers Paul McCartney.

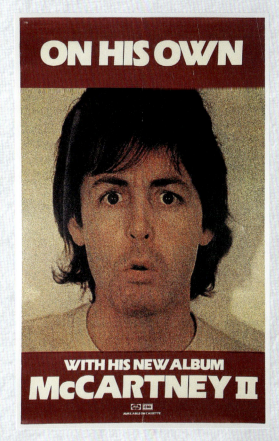

Below: Paul McCartney, 1980

Tug Of War

Released: 26 April 1982
Label: Parlophone/Capitol
Producer: George Martin
Recorded: AIR Studios, London, and Montserrat, West Indies; Park Gates Studio, Catsfield, East Sussex; Strawberry Studios South, Dorking, Surrey; Odyssey Studios, London; Hog Hill Mill, Icklesham, East Sussex
UK: No. 1
USA: No. 1

Side 1:
1. Tug of War
2. Take It Away
3. Somebody Who Cares
4. What's That You're Doing? (P McCartney/S Wonder)
5. Here Today

Side 2:
1. Ballroom Dancing
2. The Pound Is Sinking
3. Wanderlust
4. Get It
5. Be What You See (Link)
6. Dress Me Up as a Robber
7. Ebony and Ivory

This, many Paul McCartney fans celebrated with relief, was more like it – a genuinely terrific LP that restored their (and possibly his own) belief in what he was capable of as he approached 40. Just as importantly, George Martin was back at the helm along with a re-gathering of superb musicians (Stevie Wonder, guitar player Carl Perkins, bassist Stanley Clarke, drummers Steve Gadd and Dave Mattacks, Roxy Music's saxophonist Andy Mackay, 10cc's Eric Stewart, Denny Laine and, of course, Ringo Starr) to help Paul lift and maintain the high standard of musicianship throughout.

The first four numbers add up to a great opening 15 or so minutes, while 'Here Today' – a sad but heartfelt ballad in tribute to his murdered friend John Lennon – brings Side 1 to an emotional conclusion. It's true that Side 2 doesn't quite achieve the ambition of maintaining McCartney's top quality songwriting all the way through, but 'Wanderlust' has become another of his much-loved ballads, while 'Ebony and Ivory', a metaphor for racial harmony performed with Stevie Wonder, went on to be a massive hit in the UK, USA and beyond.

With at least 20 songs having been written, performed and recorded during these sessions with help from top notch British and American musicians, good news for McCartney fans, hopefully, was that there was plenty of material left over for what would become the follow-up flipside album, *Pipes of Peace*, 18 months later.

Being too big to care too much what journalists and critics say about his music, but having taken something of a battering since the huge success of *Band on the Run*, it must have felt rather warm and fuzzy for him to be able to point at evidence that he hadn't gone anywhere. Even *NME* had to admit it; as their reviewer Nick Kent put it: "...this man, only a month away from his 40th birthday, is still a contender".

Below: Paul McCartney and Stevie Wonder while recording 'Tug Of War'

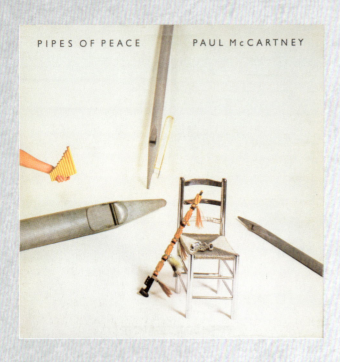

Pipes Of Peace

Released:	31 October 1983
Label:	Parlophone/Capitol
Producer:	George Martin
Recorded:	Abbey Road Studios, AIR Studios, and Odyssey Studios, London; AIR Studios, Montserrat, West Indies; Hollywood Sound, Cherokee Studios, and Westlake Recording Studios, LA; Sigma Sound Studios, NY; Park Gates Studio, Catsfield, East Sussex; Rude Studio, Campbeltown, Scotland; Hog Hill Mill, Icklesham, East Sussex; Strawberry Studios South, Dorking Surrey.
UK:	No. 4
USA:	No. 15

Side 1:
1. Pipes of Peace
2. Say Say Say (Paul McCartney/Michael Jackson)
3. The Other Me
4. Keep Under Cover
5. So Bad

Side 2:
1. The Man (Paul McCartney/Michael Jackson)
2. Sweetest Little Show
3. Average Person
4. Hey Hey (Paul McCartney/Stanley Clarke)
5. Tug of Peace
6. Through Our Love

In theory, with all of the same people involved at the same time plus Hughie Burn and Geoff Whitehorn on guitars, Nathan Watts on bass and no less than Michael Jackson providing vocals and percussion on 'Say Say Say' and 'The Man', there were high expectations that *Pipes of Peace* would at least measure up to its companion LP, *Tug of War*, but it didn't. There are some simple reasons why. First, almost all of the really good material from the sessions back in 1980-81 was used on *Tug of War*; although there were some decent numbers left over, there weren't enough. McCartney needed new material to put together a successful follow-up LP but by now he'd got himself involved in the pretty awful movie, *Give My Regards to Broad Street*, and didn't have the time or energy to devote to anything else. George Martin (who's also producing the movie soundtrack) tries to inject more soulful, perhaps even funkier production levels but, in the end, everything is delayed and enthusiasm on all sides seems to fade away.

What results is a much-awaited new album that's not really

bad, but not particularly good either. The title track is a fine opener (another UK No. 1 hit), and the two numbers with Michael Jackson are decent, pleasant pop songs of their time... and that, perhaps, is the phrase that sums up the whole thing: Eighties slushy soft pop rock was where things were. And would get worse before they got better.

While *NME* described *Pipes of Peace* as "...quasi funk and gooey rock arrangements...", *Melody Maker* twisted in the knife still further: "His songwriting has degenerated to the point where he relies either on pseudo-Stevie Wonder constructions or collaborations with Michael Jackson that spawn only wince-inducing inanities..."

Harsh, as they so often are, but it's hard not to nod gently in agreement when you consider what's coming next...

Right & Below: *Video for 'Pipes of Peace', 1984*

Press To Play

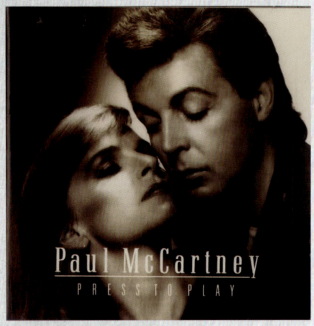

Released:	25 August 1986
Label:	Parlophone/Capitol
Producer:	Paul McCartney and Hugh Padgham
Recorded:	Hog Hill Mill Studios, Icklesham, East Sussex; Abbey Road Studios, and AIR Studios, London; Rude Studio, Campbeltown, Scotland
UK:	No. 8
USA:	No. 30

Side 1:
1. **Stranglehold** (Paul McCartney/Eric Stewart)
2. **Good Times Coming/Feel the Sun**
3. **Talk More Talk**
4. **Footprints** (Paul McCartney/Eric Stewart)
5. **Only Love Remains**

Side 2:
1. **Press**
2. **Pretty Little Head** (Paul McCartney/Eric Stewart)
3. **Move Over Busker** (Paul McCartney/Eric Stewart)
4. **Angry** (Paul McCartney/Eric Stewart)
5. **However Absurd** (Paul McCartney/Eric Stewart)

How far away can you get from a debut album by a man who was quite happy to work all by himself at home with a few instruments and a 4-track tape machine to produce his impressive, genuinely 'solo' album, and yet 15 years later, surrounds himself with a roll-call of top musos and an arsenal of flashy wiz-bang hi-tech gear that adds nothing more than flashy wiz-bang noises to a set of indescript, sterile songs? Now add a producer renowned for re-inventing drums so loud that you can't hear much else... and this, in the mid-'80s, is what you get.

The next question is, why did a man of such enormous talents as Paul McCartney allow himself to be so influenced by what was going on in the mid-'80s? The answer, I suppose, is because just about everyone else did the same thing. Whatever happened to the energy and excitement of punk and new-wave just a few years before?

There are a couple of decent numbers on *Press to Play* – the nice ballad, 'Footprints', and a genuine old rocker 'Angry', but it's not easy to find anything else that entices you to spend much time with them; much of it sounds as if it's been lifted from a Disney animation. As *Melody Maker* concluded, some of the flashy wiz-bang noises "...are rather more entertaining than the songs".

Paul admits that he doesn't like this album either and it would be three more years before he'd have another go, but this time with a new sideman who could hopefully point him in the right direction.

Discography

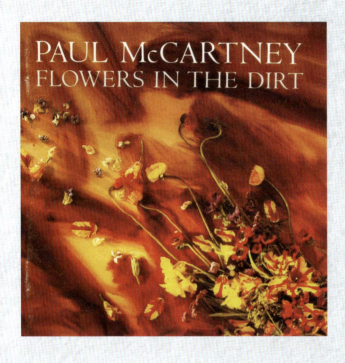

Flowers In The Dirt

Released:	5 June 1989
Label:	Parlophone/Capitol
Producer:	Paul McCartney, Mitchell Froom, Neil Dorfsman, Elvis Costello, Trevor Horn, Steve Lipson, Chris Hughes, Ross Cullum and David Foster
Recorded:	Hog Hill Mill Studios, Icklesham, East Sussex; Olympic Sound Studios, AIR Studios, Hot Nights Studios, Mayfair Studios, and Sarm West Studios, London; Mad Hatter Studios, Soundcastle Studios, and Sunset Sound Recorders, Hollywood, Los Angeles
UK:	No. 1
USA:	No. 21

Side 1:

1. **My Brave Face** (McCartney/MacManus)
2. **Rough Ride**
3. **You Want Her Too** (McCartney/MacManus)
4. **Distractions**
5. **We Got Married**
6. **Put It There**

Side 2:

1. **Figure of Eight**
2. **This One**
3. **Don't Be Careless Love** (McCartney/MacManus)
4. **That Day is Done** (McCartney/MacManus)
5. **How Many People**
6. **Motor of Love**
7. **Ou Est Le Soleil** (additional track for CD & Cassette)

So McCartney admitted *Press to Play* wasn't his finest hour and faced up to the reality that he needed to put more time and effort into the next album if things were to improve. The answer, he hoped, was not only to employ several new producers and a terrific new British band, but also to team up with a writing partner who could inspire him and have the courage to point out when things weren't going as well as they should.

His choice, of course, was the talented, fellow Liverpudlian songwriter, Declan MacManus, better known as Elvis Costello. They worked together on a number of songs in 1989 at Paul's East Sussex studio, including the co-written hit 'Veronica', about Costello's grandmother suffering from advanced Alzheimer's. One of the best songs on this album is 'That Day is Done' – a sad sequel to 'Veronica' written when Costello's grandmother passed away. Also particularly good is the very

Beatles-esque opener 'My Brave Face', released as the album's lead single.

McCartney was particularly anticipating the combination of his melodies with Costello's strength as a lyricist. It seemed the perfect solution but it's been reported that they didn't always agree, which might explain the disappointingly lush arrangements and overuse of McCartney's sometimes sticky-sweet love themes. There was also tension between Paul and one or two of his impressive team of co-producers, particularly Trevor Horn. Colleagues sticking to their guns and fighting their corner, however, were perhaps what McCartney needed; this was his best album since *Tug of War*. As *NME* put it, he was "actually competing again".

Off The Ground

Released: 2 February 1993
Label: Parlophone/Capitol
Producer: Paul McCartney and Julian Mendelsohn
Recorded: Hog Hill Mill Studios, Icklesham, East Sussex; Whitfield Street Studios (The Hit Factory), London
UK: No. 5
USA: No. 17

CD Release:

1. Off the Ground
2. Looking for Changes
3. Hope of Deliverance
4. Mistress and Maid (McCartney/MacManus)
5. I Owe It All to You
6. Biker Like an Icon
7. Peace in the Neighbourhood
8. Golden Earth Girl
9. The Lovers That Never Were (McCartney/MacManus)
10. Get Out of My Way
11. Winedark Open Sea
12. C'mon People
13. Cosmically Conscious

(hidden short track after 15 seconds silence)

McCartney had been very busy since 1989, not only working with George and Ringo putting together *The Beatles Anthology* CD collection, TV documentary and DVDs but also planning another huge world excursion, the 'New World Tour', to promote, after a four year gap, this much awaited new album. After the relative success of *Flowers in the Dirt*, he had chosen to record *Off the Ground* with the same studio and touring band (it's their feet on the cover, along with his and Linda's) that had played so well on the last album; only drummer Chris Whitten (who'd left to join Dire Straits) had been replaced by American session player Blair Cunningham.

Also still on the scene, but to a lesser degree, was Elvis Costello. Two of the best compositions on the new album – 'The Lovers That Never Were' was a leftover but a good one from the *Flowers in the Dirt* collaboration back in 1989, while 'Mistress and Maid' is believed to have been written at a follow-up writing session together in 1991.

Completely new to working with McCartney was the producer, Australian Julian Mendelsohn, perhaps best known for his work with the Pet Shop Boys and their working relationship with Dusty Springfield. McCartney wanted to rehearse the songs and then record the album in the studio as closely as possible to a live recording, in one take, in an effort to achieve a more energetic, raw feel, in keeping with the way the Beatles used to record back in the early '60s.

Any rawness that was achieved tended to get smoothed out in the production process, and McCartney's increased support for animal welfare ('Looking for Changes'), environmental issues ('Hope of Deliverance' and 'Golden Earth Girl' and world politics 'C'Mon People') left some reviewers comparing the album to "hotel elevator music". Unfair: the album includes some good numbers and the musicianship throughout is top notch, but it does lack the level of energy McCartney was aiming for.

Flaming Pie

Released: 5 May 1997
Label: Parlophone/Capitol
Producer: Paul McCartney, Jeff Lynne and George Martin
Recorded: Hog Hill Mill Studios, Icklesham, East Sussex; Abbey Road Studios, and AIR Studios, London; Steve Miller's home studio, Sun Valley, Idaho
UK: No. 2
USA: No. 2

CD Release:

1. The Song We Were Singing
2. The World Tonight
3. If You Wanna
4. Somedays
5. Young Boy
6. Calico Skies
7. Flaming Pie
8. Heaven on a Sunday
9. Used to be Bad (Paul McCartney/Steve Miller)
10. Souvenir
11. Little Willow
12. Really Love You (Paul McCartney/Richard Starkey)
13. Beautiful Night
14. Great Day

McCartney's first studio recording in over four years after his involvement in the successful *Beatles Anthology* project, the album featured several of McCartney's friends and colleagues – Ringo, George Martin, Beatles sound engineer Geoff Emerick, Jeff Lynne and Steve Miller – plus his son, James, playing guitar. With such an intimate line-up, recording the album straight after the release of the *Anthology*, it was no surprise that *Flaming Pie* (the title from Lennon's quip as to where the Beatles' name came from: "It came in a vision – a man appeared on a flaming pie and said unto them, 'from this day on you are Beatles with an 'a''") was very much an album of McCartney ballads inspired by Beatles memories. The album got underway in February 1995 when McCartney teamed up with the Electric Light Orchestra's Jeff Lynne as co-producer – a Beatles fan through and through who had already worked on the 1987 album *Cloud Nine* with his Traveling Wilburys bandmate, George Harrison, and also co-produced the new Beatles singles 'Free as a Bird' and 'Real Love' for the *Anthology*.

Below: Hog Hill Mill Studios, Icklesham

Lynne's ELO influence is clear from the outset, particularly 'If You Wanna' and 'Young Boy' and the album maintains that high standard of songwriting, production and musicianship from start to finish. Standout tracks include 'Beautiful Night' originally recorded in 1986; 'Calico Skies' (about a power cut at their home in Arizona) and the closing 'Great Day' (a little ditty he and Linda would sing together back in the early '70s) were both recorded in 1992. Why none of those songs appeared on *Off the Ground* is another good question.

Also up there are 'Used to be Bad' – a solid blues rocker co-written with Steve Miller; 'Really Love You' co-written with Ringo and the emotional 'Little Willow' written after the death of Starr's first wife, Maureen; a lovely Latin-sounding ballad 'Heaven on a Sunday' with backing vocals from Linda and son James, who also provides some nice lead guitar; the acoustic ballad 'Somedays' orchestrated beautifully by George Martin; and perhaps topping the bill, 'Souvenir', an old Beatles-style soul number with some *Abbey Road*-style heavy guitar to bring it to its conclusion.

None of the songs on this album are anything but good; there is little doubt this was McCartney's best album since *Tug of War*... and even some of those early Wings albums. Old memories would seem to have rejuvenated McCartney's slumbering talents.

Driving Rain

Released: 12 November 2001
Label: Parlophone
Producer: David Kahne
Recorded: Henson Recording Studios, Los Angeles; Madison Square Garden, and Quad Studios, New York
UK: No. 46
USA: No. 26

CD Release:
1. Lonely Road
2. From a Lover to a Friend
3. She's Given Up Talking
4. Driving Rain
5. I Do
6. Tiny Bubble
7. Magic
8. Your Way
9. **Spinning on an Axis** (Paul/James McCartney)
10. **About You**
11. **Heather**
12. **Back in the Sunshine Again** (Paul/James McCartney)
13. **Your Loving Flame**
14. **Riding into Jaipur**
15. **Rinse the Raindrops**
16. **Freedom** (hidden track)

It was four years before McCartney's next regular studio album would be released after the sad death of his wife Linda; with the desire to get back to work slowly returning, he soon had quite a few things to take care of on his 'To Do' list: his second covers album *Run Devil Run*; his second album from the Fireman, *Rushes*, along with the *Liverpool Sound Collage*, also aided by Youth; and two more classical pieces between 1997 and 1999, *Standing Stone* and *Working Classical*. Clearly he hadn't been wasting his time watching afternoon TV. Much was anticipated after the brilliant success of *Flaming Pie* – possibly it was too much to expect after so many distractions, plus the addition of a new partner, Heather Mills, to add to that list.

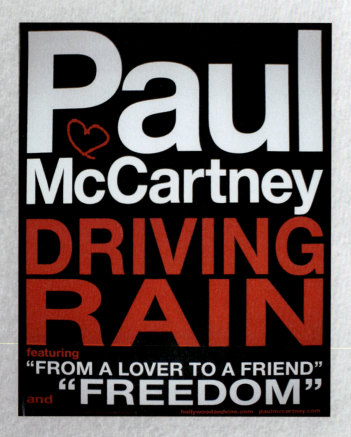

The three opening numbers, 'Lonely Road', 'From a Lover to a Friend' and 'She's Given Up Talking' are all very good and encouraged hope to continue springing eternally that this could be another excellent album out of the shadows of *Flaming Pie*. Sadly, there followed a fallow period of over 20 minutes offering little of any great interest. Then, rather surprising, retrospectively at least, there followed two of the best numbers on the album: 'About You' and the instrumental 'Heather', both written as a way of saying thank you for her help in coming to terms with Linda no longer being around.

There's an excellent number, 'Back in the Sunshine Again', co-written by McCartney and his son James, but then follows a downward spiral into another 20 minutes of relative mundanity, including another song for Heather ('Your Loving Flame'), more than 10 minutes of 'Rinse the Raindrops' and the well-meaning but painfully lacklustre 'Freedom', written by McCartney after witnessing the horror of the 9/11 attacks on New York's Twin Towers.

Somewhat surprisingly the album gained several positive reviews; *Uncut* magazine's Ian MacDonald concluded: "Possibly a grower, this album is certainly better than anything Macca's done for some while, if not the late masterpiece some of us have been hoping for."

Sales, however, were slow in the USA, and particularly the UK where it peaked no higher than No. 46 – his worst ever home market figures. This was certainly no masterpiece; if McCartney's constant desire to produce double albums had been successfully discouraged, it might have been pruned down to a much better single LP.

Discography   153

Chaos And Creation In The Backyard

Released: 12 September 2005
Label: Parlophone/Capitol
Producer: Nigel Godrich
Recorded: RAK Studios, and AIR Studios, London; Ocean Way Recording Studios, Hollywood, and Record One Recording Studios, Sherman Oaks, Los Angeles
UK: No. 10
USA: No. 6

CD Release:

1. Fine Line
2. How Kind of You
3. Jenny Wren
4. At the Mercy
5. Friends to Go
6. English Tea
7. Too Much Rain
8. A Certain Softness
9. Riding to Vanity Fair
10. Follow Me
11. Promise to You Girl
12. This Never Happened Before
13. Anyway
14. I've Only Got Two Hands (hidden instrumental track)

There are certain things that make *Chaos and Creation in the Backyard* rather different to recent previous albums. First, McCartney is reported to have been taken "out of my safety zone" to play most of the instruments himself, although there are several other musicians listed in the credits as having played their part.

The reason why he felt that way is because this was the first time since 1984's *Give My Regards to Broad Street* soundtrack (produced by George Martin) that McCartney was not credited as producer or co-producer on one of his own studio albums. This album has a connection with George Martin, too, as it was Martin who recommended Nigel Godrich to be the man in charge – well-known for his work with the likes of Radiohead, U2, R.E.M. and Beck.

Godrich's concerns about producing the album were that McCartney wouldn't be happy "to get his hands dirty" – asking if Paul would be prepared to accept the producer's sometimes forthright assessment of songs at an early stage, and either spend time making them more interesting or, alternatively, jettison them altogether. A bold approach, and it's been reported that Paul was prepared to take note, but there's little evidence that it made a huge amount of difference. Overall it's a very melodic, interesting chill-out LP with a couple of standout numbers – the acoustic ballad 'Jenny Wren' and orchestral 'Riding to Vanity Fair' (both, once again, excellent Beatles-esque songs) – but the rest of the album does rather drift along at a medium pace through to its conclusion, perhaps lacking the inventive approach for which Godrich is renowned.

Many disagree: with its unusually reflective and autobiographical approach, the album received four Grammy nominations, including one for 'Album of the Year'.

And Jon Wilde in *Uncut* magazine described *Chaos and Creation in the Backyard* as "McCartney's most sustained work of imagination and surprise since *Band on the Run*."

Despite such overall critical acclaim and high ranking in the US charts, where it stayed for 21 weeks, sales were disappointing once again in the UK, having spent just three weeks in the charts after peaking at No. 10.

Some clearly rate it very highly, others less so.

Memory Almost Full

Released: 4 June 2007
Label: Hear Music
Producer: David Kahne
Recorded: Abbey Road Studios, AIR Studios, and RAK Studios, London; Hog Hill Mill Studios, Icklesham, East Sussex; Henson Recording Studios, and Ocean Way Studios, Los Angeles

UK: No. 5
USA: No. 3

CD Release:

1. Dance Tonight
2. Ever Present Past
3. See Your Sunshine
4. Only Mama Knows
5. You Tell Me
6. Mr. Bellamy
7. Gratitude
8. Vintage Clothes
9. That Was Me
10. Feet In The Clouds
11. House Of Wax
12. The End Of The End
13. Nod Your Head

It's interesting that it was David Kahne, producer of *Driving Rain*, who was initially in charge on *Chaos and Creation in the Backyard* until the sessions were dropped and Nigel Godrich took over. Kahne, however, is back for *Memory Almost Full* two years later as he had been working on these songs back in 2003. Much of this album was actually recorded before *Chaos and Creation* and is much more the kind of material the average McCartney fan wants and expects from their hero.

Again much of the instrumentation is taken care of by Paul himself but with the support of his now well-established touring band (Rusty Anderson and Brian Ray on guitars, Paul 'Wix' Wickens on keyboards and Abe Laboriel Jr. on drums) all in place, where they remain to this day.

The album makes a great start with the last minute addition 'Dance Tonight' all the way through to 'That Was Me' without any faltering. 'Feet in the Clouds' is the first sign of a stumble and the album does tend to peter out towards the end apart from 'House of Wax', one of several unusual if not out-and-out weird numbers on the album – weird being one of McCartney's great assets in his songwriting for the Beatles and early solo material. Weird can be a good thing and just about everything on this album is very listenable and enjoyable. Terrific vocals from McCartney as well; not bad for a man just two weeks away from his 65th birthday when *Memory Almost Full* was released. Explains a lot.

The theme throughout the album, as the title suggests, is based on Paul's journey from being a Liverpool schoolboy through to a level of stardom few have ever experienced. Along with the opening number, other highlights are 'Ever Present Past' and the mini-melodrama 'Mr. Bellamy', but the entire collection of songs flows exceptionally well, offering a high level of energy, drive and Scouse humour. There are two or three numbers that perhaps should have been reconsidered, but overall this is another fine example of McCartney's canon of work during the 21st century.

As *NME*'s Alan Woodhouse put it: "This is more tuneful and exuberant than 2005's underwhelming Nigel Godrich-produced *Chaos and Creation in the Backyard*."

Just thought we'd mention that.

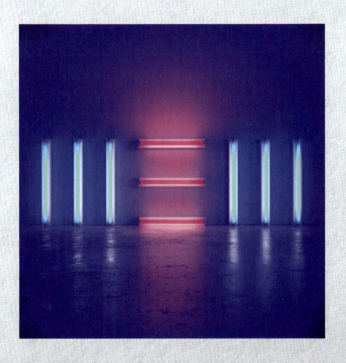

New

Released:	11 October 2013
Label:	Hear Music
Producer:	Giles Martin, Paul Epworth, Mark Ronson and Ethan Jones
Recorded:	Abbey Road Studios, AIR Studios, and Wolf Tone Studios, London; Hog Hill Mill Studios, Icklesham, East Sussex; Henson Recording Studios, Los Angeles; Avatar Studios, New York
UK:	No. 3
USA:	No. 3

CD Release:

1. **Save Us** (Paul McCartney/Paul Epworth)
2. **Alligator**
3. **On My Way to Work**
4. **Queenie Eye** (Paul McCartney/Paul Epworth)
5. **Early Days**
6. **New**
7. **Appreciate**
8. **Everybody Out There**
9. **Hosanna**
10. **I Can Bet**
11. **Looking at Her**
12. **Road** (Paul McCartney/Paul Epworth)
13. **Scared** (hidden track)

Another first for McCartney with an album of all-new songs put together with the help of four young producers he particularly admired. Initially he intended to try them out for a short period before selecting the one he considered most appropriate to record the album. He ended up working with all four: Giles Martin, son of George, as executive producer, plus Mark Ronson, Ethan Johns and Paul Epworth. McCartney was hoping that this group of young talent would be able to provide the more modern sound he was looking for – something "new", hence the title – to balance out the 71 years he had existed on this planet, writing music almost all of that time. Some of the songs reflect those years before he became a member of the world's most famous band, others looking towards the time he'll sadly no longer be with us.

Mark Ronson had been chosen after DJ-ing at McCartney's wedding to his third wife, Nancy Shevell, in 2011; "... a happy period in my life" as Paul described it, resulting in "new songs when you get a new woman". The two songs Ronson recorded for the album – 'Alligator' and the title love song 'New' – are among the best numbers on the album.

Once again several tracks are autobiographical: 'On My Way to Work' (produced by Giles Martin) concerns the time he worked as a driver's mate for a delivery company in Liverpool. In 'Early Days' (Ethan Johns) Paul reminisces about his youthful relationship in Liverpool with John Lennon listening to songs in a local record store. Producer Paul Epworth's 'Queenie Eye' is based on a school playground game Paul played as a child, while the opening track 'Save Us' is also one of the highlights.

McCartney's attempt to march confidently into his eighth decade of music-making surrounded by such relatively youthful production talent was met with praise from many media critics: *Rolling Stone*'s Will Hermes commented that "*New* feels energised and full of joyous rock and roll invention. More than a sentimental journey, it's an album that wants to be part of the 21st-century pop dialogue."

The *Daily Telegraph*'s Helen Brown reached a similar conclusion, drawing attention to McCartney's "fresh attitude" compared to his more introspective *Memory Almost Full* six years earlier: "Though they're produced by men young enough to be his sons, these 12 songs are vintage Macca ... this album proves his talent is timeless."

Few would argue, but one question remains: would the more orthodox approach of just the one talented young producer have resulted in a more cohesive album?

Discography 157

Egypt Station

Released:	7 September 2018
Label:	Capitol
Producer:	Greg Kurstin, Ryan Tedder and Paul McCartney
Recorded:	Henson Recording Studios, Patriot Studios, Emmanuel Presbyterian Church, and EastWest Studios, Los Angeles; Hog Hill Mill Studios, Icklesham, East Sussex; Abbey Road Studios, London; Uno Mas, Brentwood, Tennessee, USA; KLB Studios, Sao Paulo, Brazil
UK:	No. 3
USA:	No. 1

Side 1:
1. Opening Station (Link)
2. I Don't Know
3. Come On to Me
4. Happy With You

Side 2:
1. Who Cares
2. Fuh You (Paul McCartney/Ryan Tedder)
3. Confidante
4. People Want Peace
5. Hand In Hand

Side 3:
1. Dominoes
2. Back In Brazil
3. Do It Now
4. Caesar Rock

Side 4:
1. Despite Repeated Warnings
2. Station II (Link)
3. Hunt You Down/Naked/C-Link

Back with Capitol Records five years after the release of *New*, the question was how much newer than *New* could McCartney get, and why would he want to at the age of 76? Because he's Paul McCartney.

Co-produced by Greg Kurstin (known for his work with Adele, Beck and the Foo Fighters, among others) plus one track co-produced by Ryan Tedder (lead vocalist for the US rock band OneRepublic) *Egypt Station* represents another typically huge McCartney project. He described it as "a loose concept" album with the song cycle starting off at the station in Egypt before heading off to a succession of other locations on which the compositions are based. A double concept album. With no less than 16 different 'locations'. Does it work? It does, actually, rather well.

Of the 14 actual songs (two are simply short instrumental links), 'I Don't Know' is one of McCartney's best ballads for sometime; 'Happy with You' conveys how maturity brings modern day contentedness, sung in a wise old Johnny Cash-style that perfectly suits his, at times, wavering vocals. 'Who Cares' is a solid blues rocker dealing with bullying; 'Confident' expresses regrets that a relationship (actually with his guitar, he says) had faltered; 'Hand in Hand' is a lovely piano ballad about making future plans in later life; 'Dominoes' considers small actions having big impacts; 'Back in Brazil' is a lively Latin dance number set (and recorded) in Sao Paulo; while 'Do it Now' is another lovely slow ballad advising us all to seize the day... all in all, an impressive collection of songs among the most enlightening, revealing and catchy material McCartney has produced for some time.

It draws towards journey-end with the equally impressive 'Despite Repeated Warnings', an episodic melodrama in which McCartney expresses his views on global warming, with Donald Trump portrayed as a mad sea captain intent on driving his vessel onto the rocks. Written in the Beatles or early Wings approach of three separate sections linked as a 7-minute plus epic, McCartney gets his message across very aptly. Finally, a Beatles-esque medley of 'Hunt You Down/ Naked/C-Link' works well as a three-song finale to bring *Egypt Station* to the final destiny on its fascinating journey.

Unlikely that Trump rushed out to buy a copy but *Egypt Station* debuted at No. 1 in America – his first US album topping the charts since *Tug of War* in 1982. It didn't do too badly in the UK either, climbing to No. 3. A 76-year-old man producing a double 'concept' album genuinely reflecting his mature emotions and abundant talents was something to celebrate in 2018. Even the album title and cover artwork had been created by McCartney back in 1988. Another 30 years had done little to diminish his remarkable career.

McCartney III

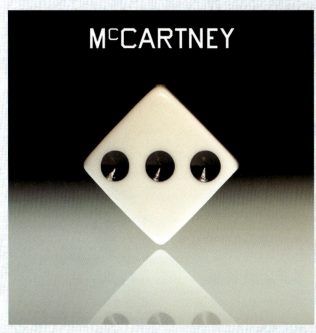

Released:	18 December 2020
Label:	Capitol
Producer:	Paul McCartney, Greg Kurstin and George Martin
Recorded:	Hog Hill Mill Studios, Icklesham, East Sussex
UK:	No. 1
USA:	No. 2

Side 1:
1. Long Tailed Winter Bird
2. Find My Way
3. Pretty Boys
4. Women and Wives
5. Lavatory Lil'
6. Deep Deep Feeling

Side 2:
7. Slidin'
8. The Kiss of Venus
9. Seize the Day
10. Deep Down
11. Winter Bird/When Winter Comes

With McCartney's career on a roll after the critical and chart success of *Egypt Station* and the announcement that he would be headlining Saturday night at 2020's Glastonbury Festival, it seemed nothing could go wrong for him. And then, as none of us expected, along came Covid-19 and everything fell apart. Most people used the time to work on those annoying little jobs around the house that had needed doing for years, and McCartney was no different. Thirty years after *McCartney II*, he decided to make *McCartney III*.

Coming up to the age of 78, and with long life-expectancy suddenly something none of us could take for granted anymore, questions were being asked: might this be a fitting swansong for a man approaching the end of a remarkable, six-decade, solo career – his third genuine one-man band album 50 years after the first effort back in 1970? Probably not. Sir Paul just got on with it.

McCartney III was recorded (as if he had any choice) at Hog Hill Mill Studios in the early part of 2020 with Paul using the time to make music for himself: "I just did stuff I fancied doing. I had no idea this would end up as an album," he said. He began by recording whichever instrument the song had been written on and then added more layers, playing everything himself apart from 'Slidin'' (written during the Winter Olympics) with some of the drum and guitar parts performed by his band during the *Egypt Station* sessions.

As with both of his previous eponymous titles, the first listening is certainly not easy listening and the opening 'Long Tailed Winter Bird', with its five-minute-plus repetitive acoustic guitar riff, might concern some fans as to where the rest of this album might be going, but it goes pretty well. From that point on is a succession of decent material with three outstanding numbers: 'Women and Wives' in tribute to the blues singer Lead Belly; the eight-minute love song 'Deep Deep Feeling'; and the beautiful acoustic ballad 'Winter Bird/When Winter Comes' (originally recorded in 1992 with George Martin as producer) recalling Paul's hippy existence on his Scottish farm back in the Seventies and bringing an enjoyable 40 minutes to a happy conclusion.

As with all of Paul's *McCartney* albums, this one joins the 'love or hate' collection, which Mark Beaumont's review in *NME* summed up perfectly: "Where *McCartney III* really breaks from the lineage of its eponymous forebears is in its sheer unpredictability. A 'White Album' sort of eclecticism was key to the greatness of 2018's *Egypt Station*, and *McCartney III* is even more chameleonic." Listen to it, if you haven't already, and you'll know exactly what he means.

The album debuted at No. 1 in the UK on Christmas Day during that lockdown year – his first No. 1 solo album at home since *Flowers in the Dirt*. In the US, the album debuted at No. 2 to make him the first artist to have a new album at either No. 1 or No. 2 in the chart in each of the last six decades. The word, once again, is remarkable.

McCartney III imagined:

Another McCartney-approved tribute album released by Capitol Records in 2021 featuring new versions of songs from *McCartney III* recorded by a variety of musicians described as: "friends, fans and brand new acquaintances". The list includes Beck, Dominic Fike, Khruangbin, St. Vincent, Dev Hynes, Phoebe Bridgers, Ed O'Brien, Damon Albarn, Josh Homme and Robert Del Naja. Made it to the Top 20 in both the UK and USA.

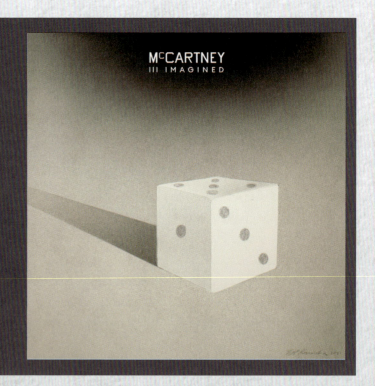

Right: For the third time, Paul McCartney headlines Glastonbury Festival (on 25 June 2022) – the oldest ever headline act on the Pyramid Stage at the age of 80

Discography | 161

Paul McCartney/Wings original studio albums

from worst to best?

22 **.Press To Play** (1986)
Paul had got his hands on various boxes of shiny techno kit to make weird noises that add nothing (the opposite, in fact) to a collection of largely indifferent songs. Even he openly admits this isn't very good.

21 **.McCartney II** (1980)
Experimental is the kindest word for this follow-up one-man-band album 10 years after the impressive *McCartney*. Three or four great songs squeezed in among a crazy synth mess makes this difficult for some people to listen to or like.

20 **.Driving Rain** (2001)
A double album, in effect, it starts so well but then tails off and, apart from a resurgence midway, drags on for far too long. Better editing and production would have made this a much more satisfying single album.

19 **.New** (2013)
McCartney makes a move into his eighth decade looking both forward and back with the assistance of four talented young producers employed to guide him through his attempt to find something new to say. Would just one young opinion have helped produce something more coherent and... better?

18 **.Chaos And Creation In The Backyard** (2005)
More inventive than many of Paul's solo albums before *Flaming Pie*, this is a fine example of those Beatles-esque, often autobiographical ballads that define his talent but, in the last 20 years or so, have sometimes been lacking in comparable levels of depth. Interesting, but not everyone's English cup of tea.

17 **.McCartney III** (2020)
There was much hope this would be Paul's very worthy solo swansong following the success of *Egypt Station* and it very nearly succeeds, but the good stuff has to be dug out from among some more examples of McCartney's one-man wackiness that not everyone appreciates.

16 **.Back To The Egg** (1979)
A more basic, punk-influenced attempt to get down with the kids, this is the weakest of the Wings albums, lacking hooks and with no really memorable numbers that stand out. McCartney had basically lost interest, Laine quit, and the band's 10-year lifespan (or Wingspan) came to an end.

15 **.Memory Almost Full** (2007)
Much of this was actually recorded before 2005's *Chaos and Creation in the Backyard*

Discography

but this re-employed the original *Chaos and Creation* producer David Kahne (rather than Nigel Godrich) and many feel he did a better job. Probably McCartney's best 21st century album until *Egypt Station* arrived 11 years later.

14. London Town (1978)
Paul's Seventies folk album, the best material is co-written with Denny Laine but, overall, the album lacks cohesion or any recognisable theme. Perhaps not a good idea to name it after foggy London Town and record it on a yacht in the Virgin Islands...

13. Pipes Of Peace (1983)
In effect a follow-up to *Tug of War* mostly recorded at the same time with predominantly the same line-up, although George Martin's approach as producer was to try to make this a funkier, more soulful companion LP. Some works well, but overall it's short of material of the same high quality as *Tug of War*.

12. Off The Ground (1993)
A decent album that improves with each play but doesn't quite achieve the level of energy McCartney was seeking by recording most of the songs live in the studio. His choice of controversial subjects (politics, environment, animal welfare etc) also rubbed some fans and critics up the wrong way.

11. Flowers In The Dirt (1989)
McCartney's songwriting partnership with Elvis Costello promised so much and their four co-written numbers are among the best on Paul's first album specifically designed for CD (released the following year). Lyrically and musically, at times, disappointingly lightweight, but overall a huge improvement over 1986's *Press to Play*.

10. Wild Life (1971)
Much better than most reviews seem to give it credit for. No fillers or disasters but only one real show stopper held back almost to the very end: 'Dear Friend'. Improves if given more time, Wings' debut is actually not bad at all.

9. McCartney (1970)
Some of these songs could easily have appeared on *Abbey Road*, but overall there are a few too many instrumental fillers, which is a shame. He needed to get it out quickly but more patience could have resulted in his best ever solo album. As it is, good+ combined with elements of brilliance.

8. Egypt Station (2018)
Not really a concept album, more of a themed double album visiting a variety of locations and emotions in older life, physically, mentally and politically. Expressing his feelings and beliefs incredibly well, this was McCartney's best comeback album since '97's *Flaming Pie*. Not bad for a 76-year-old.

7. Red Rose Speedway (1973)
Another example of a Wings album that often gets slated but is actually pretty good. Some great songs while Henry McCullough's improvised guitar solo on 'My Love' by itself makes the entrance ticket worth the fee.

6. Tug Of War (1982)
George Martin is back in charge and doesn't it show. Side 1 is up there with Paul's better Wings material. Side 2 doesn't quite maintain that standard all the way through but, overall, a terrific LP that renewed belief in Paul's talent as he approached the ripe old age of 40.

5. Wings At The Speed Of Sound (1976)

Another much underrated album that's often described as a stopgap, but is so much more than that. This is the direction in which Wings should have been heading – Paul's capabilities benefitting from Denny Laine and Jimmy McCulloch's songwriting contributions. Sadly, it was not to be.

4. Flaming Pie (1997)

With help and input from the likes of Jeff Lynne, Steve Miller and George Martin, this is McCartney's best Beatles-esque ballads album. More than 25 years after the band split, *Flaming Pie* regenerates critical recognition (with much-needed help from other music maestros) of Paul's songwriting genius as a solo artist.

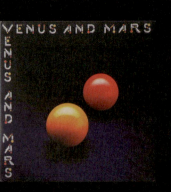

3. Venus And Mars (1975)

A perfect example of a big band attempting to follow-up a classic predecessor. So many fail, but Wings succeed brilliantly. Not a single bad track and a level of energy throughout that reminds everyone that Paul and his band are good old-fashioned rockers at heart.

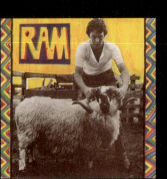

2. RAM (1971)

The album that could have at least contributed to his debut solo LP if there'd been more time. No better evidence that Paul has come out the other side of his dark depression to remind the world, with Linda's help, how brilliant he is. A wonderfully funny, engrossing, entertaining collection of folky pop songs.

Discography 165

1. Band On The Run (1973)

Easily the best Wings album, one of Paul's most impressive pieces of work and up there among the great albums of the Seventies. A perfect example of the finest artistic achievements often being produced under difficult circumstances; despite his band jumping ship at the final hour, he flies to Lagos with Linda and Donny (where they get mugged!) to create his post-Beatles masterpiece. A doddle.

Paul McCartney/Wings Live Albums

Wings Over America

Released:	10 December 1976
Label:	Capitol
Producer:	Paul McCartney
Recorded:	Various venues in the USA and Abbey Road Studios, London
UK:	No. 8
USA:	No. 1

Recorded during the US leg of their 1975-76 'Wings Over the World Tour', primarily at the Forum near Los Angeles. Over 800 hours of live performances were recorded and it was left to McCartney to choose the final tracks for the triple album from five best versions of each number selected by his engineers. Five Beatles songs are included ('Yesterday', 'Lady Madonna', 'I've Just Seen a Face', 'Blackbird' and 'The Long and Winding Road), which, for the first time, are credited as McCartney-Lennon, rather than the usual reverse order.

Concerts For The People Of Kampuchea

Released:	30 March 1981
Label:	Atlantic
Producer:	Chris Thomas
Recorded:	Hammersmith Odeon, London
UK:	Did not chart
USA:	No. 36

A live double album recorded at concerts over four days in December 1979 to raise money for war-torn Cambodia, organised by McCartney and the Secretary-General of the United Nations, Austrian politician Kurt Waldheim. Performers include Queen, the Who, Ian Dury and the Blockheads, the Pretenders and the Clash, while Wings performed on the final night (supported by Rockpile and Elvis Costello and the Imposters). The climax was McCartney's concept of Rockestra, a supergroup featuring Wings and 30-plus rock stars including members of the Who, Led Zeppelin, the Faces and Pink Floyd taking up Side 4.

Tripping The Live Fantastic

Released:	5 November 1990
Label:	Parlophone
Producer:	Paul McCartney, Bob Clearmountain and Peter Henderson
Recorded:	Various venues across Europe, the USA and Brazil
UK:	No. 17
USA:	No. 26

McCartney's first live solo album and first complete live album for almost 14 years since *Wings Over America*. This triple album made up of performances from his successful 'Paul McCartney World Tour' navigates through his entire Beatles, Wings and solo material right up to 1989's *Flowers in the Dirt*. It is noticeable, however, that all Beatles songs included return to being credited as Lennon-McCartney. A single *Highlights!* version of the album was also released that year but failed to chart in the UK or USA.

Unplugged (The Official Bootleg)

Released:	20 May 1991
Label:	Parlophone
Producer:	Paul McCartney
Recorded:	London Limehouse TV Studios
UK:	No. 7
USA:	No. 14

Following his hugely successful 'Paul McCartney World Tour' he made the decision to strip down to the bone a few Beatles numbers and some of his favourite songs from the Fifties and Sixties, performing them unplugged, with acoustic instruments, on the by now very popular *MTV Unplugged* American cable TV show. Very well received, the show is also available as a Deluxe edition with a double CD and live performance DVD. Highly recommended.

Discography

Paul Is Live

Released: 8 November 1993
Label: Parlophone
Producer: Paul McCartney
Recorded: Various venues in the USA and Australia
UK: No. 34
USA: No. 78

Recorded during the 1993 'New World Tour' in support of his album *Off the Ground*, *Paul is Live* (as before) works its way through McCartney's Beatles, Wings and solo days with the addition of a couple of Forties/Fifties rockers and a short two-minute piece in tribute to Chet Atkins, performed solo by guitarist Robbie McIntosh. The title of the album is a reference to the 'Paul is dead' rumours after the release of the Beatles' 1969 album *Abbey Road*. The cover shot is from the same photo session for *Abbey Road* but manipulated using computer software.

Back In The Us: Live 2002

Released: 11 November 2002
Label: Capitol
Producer: David Kahne
Recorded: Various venues in the USA
UK: Not released
USA: No. 8

The first Paul McCartney album not to be released on vinyl, this was an exclusive US and Japan (where it reached No. 4) double CD live album supporting his 2001 release *Driving Rain*, recorded

Below: Paul McCartney and Pete Townshend of the Who, followed by Led Zeppelin's John Paul Jones, enjoying some roister-doistering as they leave the stage after the Rockestra's performance at the Concerts for the People of Kampuchea, London's Hammersmith Odeon, 29th December 1979

on the following year's 'Driving USA Tour'. Not surprisingly the album once again features a majority of Beatles numbers plus solo material with and without Wings; only four numbers are actually taken from the *Driving Rain* album. Interestingly, once again Paul reversed the song credits of Beatles numbers to 'Paul McCartney and John Lennon', which infuriated Yoko Ono and resulted in the threat of legal action.

Back In The World: Live

Released:	17 March 2003
Label:	Parlophone
Producer:	David Kahne
Recorded:	Various venues in the US, Japan and Mexico
UK:	No. 5
USA:	Not released

Basically the same album as *Back in the US*, this double CD was released four months later for the European market. The first discs on both versions are identical apart from one song, 'Vanilla Sky', being dropped from the 'World' release; two tracks from the 'US' Disc 2 ('C-Moon' and 'Freedom' are replaced with four other songs ('Calico Skies', 'Michelle', 'Let 'Em In' and 'She's Leaving Home') on the 'World' release. Some of the material on this 'World' album also features alternative recordings from concerts in Japan and Mexico. Live DVDs of both the 'US' and 'World' releases are also available.

Good Evening New York City

Released:	17 November 2009
Label:	Hear Music
Producer:	Paul McCartney
Recorded:	Citi Field, New York
UK:	No. 28
USA:	No. 16

A double CD (and DVD) live album recorded over three nights as the first ever performances at Citi Field, the new home of the New York Mets baseball team, and close to the site of the Mets' previous Shea Stadium where the Beatles had set record concert attendance figures in 1965. George Harrison's 'Something' is performed solo by Paul playing a ukulele (as a tribute to the late Harrison as a member of the George Formby Society) and, despite Yoko's previous livid threats of legal action, all other Beatles songs on the album are credited as McCartney/Lennon apart from 'Day Tripper' and 'A Day in the Life', which revert to the original partnership listing. McCartney also performs Lennon's 'Give Peace a Chance' in tribute to John.

Amoeba Gig

Released:	12 July 2019
Label:	Capitol
Producer:	Darrell Thorp, David Kahne and Bob Ludwig
Recorded:	Amoeba Music, Hollywood, California
UK:	No. 82
USA:	Did not chart

Lifted from a secret performance in front of just a few hundred fans on 27 June 2007 at a large record store in California, to promote the album *Memory Almost Full*, the recordings were originally released in November 2007 as *Amoeba's Secret*, a limited edition 12-inch vinyl record, with a CD version added in 2009. In 2010 it was released once again in the UK and Ireland as *Live in Los Angeles,* offered as a free gift by the *Mail on Sunday* and *Irish Sunday Mail* national newspapers. An extended CD version was made available in 2012 only to premium members of the McCartney website. It was not until July 2019 that a remixed version of the complete show was finally released to the public on CD, vinyl, and as a digital download. (One point of interest is that this was the first McCartney album since 1989 not to feature on keyboards Paul 'Wix' Wickens, who was reported to be back in the UK organising a tribute concert in memory of Princess Diana. He was replaced by Dave Arch – now better known as the musical director and arranger on the BBC TV show *Strictly Come Dancing...*)

Soundtracks, Covers & Curiosities

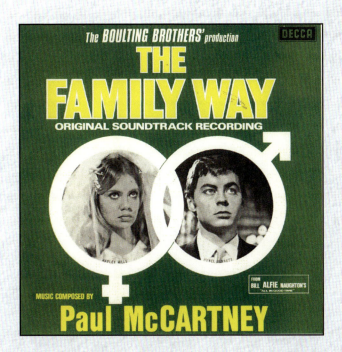

The Family Way
(George Martin Orchestra)

Released:	6 January 1967
Label:	Decca/London
Producer:	George Martin
Recorded:	CTS Studios, London
UK:	Did not chart
USA:	Did not chart

Music composed by Paul McCartney for the 1966 film *The Family Way*, directed by Roy Boulting and starring Hywel Bennett, Hayley Mills and her father John Mills. The music was arranged by George Martin and performed by the George Martin Orchestra. Just 25 minutes in length but a perfect example of beautiful flute-drenched melodies for British, Sixties, kitchen sink drama. No doubt Paul had a great deal of help from George Martin, but still a wonderful piece of work for someone with no real experience of film composition.

Live And Let Die
(George Martin With Wings)

Released:	2 July 1973
Label:	United Artists
Producer:	George Martin
Recorded:	AIR Studios, London
UK:	Did not chart
USA:	Did not chart

McCartney had been considered to write the title song for the previous James Bond film *Diamonds Are Forever*, scored as usual by John Barry, but who was unavailable for the next Bond movie, *Live and Let Die*, the film producers Harry Saltzman and Albert Broccoli approached McCartney with the idea of writing the theme song. Paul asked George Martin to record it – the first time they had worked together since the Beatles' *Abbey Road* album in 1969. Written by Paul and Linda and performed by Wings, so impressed were Saltzman and Broccoli when they heard the single that they then asked Martin to handle the entire film soundtrack's score and orchestration. Working closely with the film's director Guy Hamilton, the soundtrack was recorded at Martin's AIR Studios in Oxford Street, London and the theme song went on to become the first Bond theme to be nominated for an Oscar for 'Best Original Song' (losing to Barbra Streisand's 'The Way We Were').

McGear
(Mike McGear With Wings)

Released:	24 September 1974
Label:	Warner Bros.
Producer:	Paul McCartney
Recorded:	Strawberry Studios, Stockport, and Abbey Road Studios, London
UK:	Did not chart
USA:	Did not chart

The second solo album of Paul's brother, Peter Michael McCartney, better known as a member of the comedy band the Scaffold under the stage name Mike McGear. Six of the songs on the album were co-written by Mike, Paul and Linda, two just by Paul and Linda with a further song written with Roger McGough, one of Mike's bandmates in the Scaffold. All five members of Wings at the time (Paul and Linda with Denny Laine, Jimmy McCulloch and Denny Seiwell) perform on the album – well worth tracking down.

Thrillington (Percy 'Thrills' Thrillington)

Released:	29 April 1977
Label:	Regal Zonophone/Capitol
Producer:	Paul McCartney
Recorded:	Abbey Road Studios, London
UK:	Did not chart
USA:	Did not chart

These easy listening versions of the songs from *Ram* were recorded in June 1971 with Paul as producer but not performer, and arrangements by Richard Hewson who worked on the orchestration before *Ram* had been released. When Wings were formed, however, the decision was made to shelve the project. It was not until 1976 that Paul decided to release the album but disguising his own involvement in the liner notes (written by himself under the pseudonym Clint Harrigan and describing Paul as a friend of the fictitious Percy Thrillington). On release, even with advertisements taken out in the *London Evening Standard* newspaper, it disappeared without seeming to thrill anyone. Now an expensive collector's item.

Give My Regards To Broad Street

Released:	22 October 1984
Label:	Parlophone/Columbia
Producer:	George Martin
Recorded:	Abbey Road Studios, AIR Studios, CTS Studios, and Elstree Film Studios, London
UK:	No. 1
USA:	No. 21

Where does one begin with this – the soundtrack to what is in all honesty a pretty dreadful movie? In effect a compilation of some of McCartney's greatest Beatles songs ('Yesterday', 'Here, There and Everywhere', 'Good Day Sunshine' and 'Eleanor Rigby' with an extended orchestral section arranged by George Martin) plus solo and Wings numbers and three new tracks: 'No More Lonely Nights', 'Not Such a Bad Boy' and 'No Values'. Most of the music, of course, is magnificent (although the sound montage is not the best way to hear these Beatles classics) but when it's all been put together for a film that is generally considered a turkey, one can only tend to agree with *New Musical Express* when they described the whole thing as "a pointless exercise".

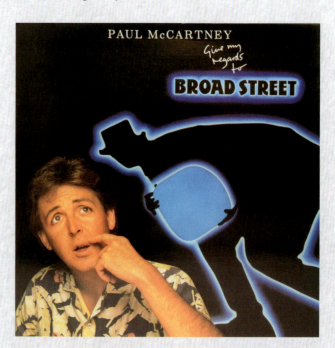

Choba A CCCP

Released:	31 October 1988 (USSR)/29 October 1991 rest of world
Label:	Melodiya
Producer:	Paul McCartney
Recorded:	Hog Hill Mill Studios, Icklesham, East Sussex
UK:	No. 63
USA:	Did not chart

Translated as 'Back Again in the USSR', this classic rock 'n' roll covers album of songs from the Twenties through to the Sixties was originally released for the Russian market only, but eventually made available elsewhere three years later. In the USSR it sold over 400,000 copies in its first year of release.

Run Devil Run

Released:	4 October 1999
Label:	Parlophone
Producer:	Paul McCartney and Chris Thomas
Recorded:	Abbey Road Studios, London
UK:	No. 12
USA:	No. 27

A second largely Fifties rock 'n' roll covers album plus three original McCartney numbers – the title track plus 'Try Not to Cry' and 'What It Is' – all written in dedication to his wife Linda. Paul recorded the album a year after her death as a way of getting back to work and celebrating the sort of songs he (and she) loved and grew up with. A live performance in support of the album took place at the Cavern Club in Liverpool in December 1999.

Kisses On The Bottom

Released:	6 February 2012
Label:	Hear Music
Producer:	Tommy LiPuma
Recorded:	Capitol Studios, Los Angeles, and Avatar Studios, New York
UK:	No. 3
USA:	No. 5

His third covers album concentrates largely on traditional US numbers from the Twenties, Thirties and Forties but with the addition of two original McCartney songs, 'My Valentine' (dedicated to his new wife Nancy Shevell) and 'Only Our Hearts'. An extended Deluxe edition of the album with four additional songs and live versions of the original numbers was released for the UK/US markets in November 2012.

Compilations

Wings Greatest

Released:	22 November 1978
Label:	Parlophone/Capitol
UK:	No. 5
USA:	No. 29

The first Wings compilation and the first McCartney retrospective since the Beatles' split, it offers an excellent overview of Paul's solo career from 1970 through to '78. Ten Wings numbers are included from the albums *Red Rose Speedway*, *Band on the Run*, *Wings at the Speed of Sound* and *London Town* (although not *Venus and Mars* for some strange reason), plus two singles 'Live and Let Die' and 'Mull of Kintyre', and two solo numbers, 'Another Day' and (with Linda, from the album *Ram*), 'Uncle Albert/Admiral Halsey'.

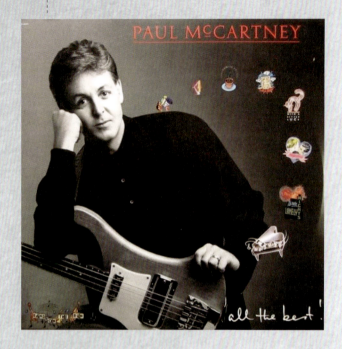
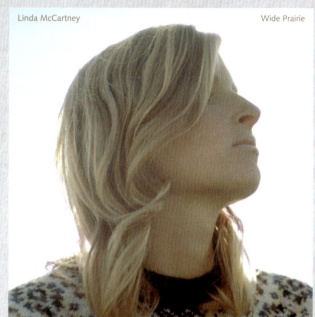

All The Best!

Released:	2 November 1987
Label:	Parlophone/Capitol
UK:	No. 2
USA:	No. 62

The album contains tracks from the beginning of his solo career in 1970 up to (outside the US) the newly recorded single 'Once Upon a Long Ago'. Released just as McCartney was beginning work on his next major studio album *Flowers in the Dirt*, this compilation was a commercial success in the UK but, despite Capitol selecting different tracks reflecting their popularity in the US, the album proved strangely less successful in America where it peaked at No. 62. Nonetheless, it sold almost 1 million copies in the UK and over 2 million in the USA.

Linda's posthumous compilation album, released just six months after her death, is made up of material recorded between 1972 and 1998 at various locations around the world. Paul was inspired to put the album together after a fan wrote to him asking about the track 'Seaside Woman', recorded by Wings but released as a single under the name Suzy and the Red Stripes. (The track made it into the UK charts at No. 90 and to No. 59 in the US Hot 100; it also appeared on the original double album version of Wings' *Red Rose Speedway*.) Every member of Wings appears on the album apart from drummers Geoff Britton and Steve Holley. Of the 17 songs on the album, Linda had written five by herself, six with Paul, two with Paul and Carla Lane, and one with Mick Bolton of Mott the Hoople (the remaining three tracks were covers). Two tracks from the album were released as singles – 'Wild Prairie' made it to No. 74 while 'The Light Comes From Within' reached No. 56 in the UK charts.

Wide Prairie (Linda McCartney)

Released:	26 October 1998
Label:	Capitol
Producer:	Paul and Linda McCartney, Lee Perry and Ian Maidman
UK:	Did not chart
USA:	Did not chart

Wingspan: Hits And History

Released:	7 May 2001
Label:	Parlophone
UK:	No. 5
USA:	No. 2

Another excellent solo and Wings career overview from 1970's *McCartney* all the way through to 1984's *Give My Regards to Broad Street*. This double CD compilation is separated into two sets: 'Hits' made up of 18 numbers that all made it into the Top 10 in either the UK/US or both, while 'History' provides 22 lesser-known songs of the same period, including one previously unreleased number 'Bip Bop/ Hey Diddle' from the *Ram* sessions in 1971. The album was linked to a TV documentary of the same name produced by his daughter Mary; she interviews her father to discuss the breakup of the Beatles, his marriage to her mother and his solo career and as a member of Wings. The film *Wingspan* can now be found on DVD.

Pure McCartney

Released:	10 June 2016
Label:	Concord Music Group
UK:	No. 9
USA:	No. 15

McCartney's first solo compilation for 15 years, the double CD, 4-disc vinyl LP or Deluxe 4-disc CD (or digital version) includes tracks from all of his official studio albums except *Choba B CCCP*, *Flowers in the Dirt*, *Run Devil Run* and *Driving Rain*. Most of the tracks on *Pure McCartney* are Top 40 hits.

Boxsets

Paul McCartney: The CD Collection

Released:	1989
Label:	UFO

A boxset for the US market to promote 'The Paul McCartney World Tour', containing his nine solo albums (not including Wings material) from *McCartney* to *Flowers in the Dirt*, including the *All the Best!* compilation album. The box has 10 slots for the nine CDs plus a colour photo book including tour information and setlist. Can be found online but doesn't come up very often.

The Paul McCartney Collection

Released:	7 June 1993
Label:	Parlophone

A series of 16 remastered CDs of McCartney's solo and Wings albums, plus bonus tracks. The albums in the collection were released separately, with the first eight (from *McCartney* to *London Town*) released on 7 June 1993, and the second eight (*Wings Greatest* to *Flowers in the Dirt*) on 9 August that year.

Wings 1971-73

Released:	7 December 2018
Label:	Capitol

Released as part of McCartney's Archive Collection, this boxset contains deluxe versions of reissues of *Wild Life* and *Red Rose Speedway* and a new live album *Wings Over Europe* recorded during the 'Wings Over Europe Tour', exclusive to the boxset. Additional material includes a 96-page 'Wings Over Europe Tour' photo book and a facsimile of the 1972 tour programme.

McCartney I II III

Released:	5 August 2022
Label:	Capitol/MPL/UMC

Made up of McCartney's three eponymous solo albums recorded in 1970, 1980 and 2020 primarily at his home studios in Cavendish Avenue, London; High Park Farm in Scotland; and in both Peasmarsh and Icklesham, East Sussex. Released both on CD and limited edition black or coloured vinyl.

The 7" Singles Box

Released:	2 December 2022
Label:	MPL

No less than 80 McCartney singles (amounting to 163 songs) released between 1971 to 2022, remastered at Abbey Road, loaded into a wooden crate of which only 3000 were available worldwide, and released shortly after Sir Paul's headlining performance at Glastonbury. Not a bad way to celebrate your 80th birthday. Needless to say, *The 7" Singles Box* sold out almost immediately, despite the considerable price attached of almost £500 or just over $600. It even made it into the Billboard 200 at No. 126. Of the 80 singles, 15 had never been released on 7-inch vinyl before, while the box also includes one EP, one exclusive randomly selected test pressing, and a 148-page book containing a foreword by Paul, an essay written by *Rolling Stone*'s Rob Sheffield, plus recording notes and chart information on each of the singles.

Classical Albums

Liverpool Oratorio (With Carl Davis)

Released:	7 October 1991
Label:	EMI Classics
Producer:	John Fraser
Recorded:	Liverpool Cathedral
UK:	No. 36
USA:	Did not chart

McCartney's first serious attempt at classical music, composed in collaboration with conductor Carl Davis to commemorate the Royal Liverpool Philharmonic Orchestra's 150th anniversary. Featuring the New Zealand opera singer Dame Kiri Te Kanawa, the oratorio was recorded at a dress rehearsal and premiered at Liverpool's Anglican Cathedral and is made-up of eight movements loosely based on a life story similar to his own. Not particularly well-received by the media, the album nonetheless made its way to the top of various classical charts around the world and No. 36 in the UK Official Albums Chart.

Standing Stone

Released:	25 September 1997
Label:	EMI Classics
Producer:	John Fraser
Recorded:	Abbey Road Studios
UK:	No. 34
USA:	Did not chart

McCartney's second classical composition was his first purely instrumental piece involving no libretto, although a 120-member choir was employed alongside the 80 musicians from the London Symphony Orchestra conducted by Lawrence Foster. Despite no lyrics as such, the piece was based on a McCartney poem considering how early Celtic man (dating from around 700 BC) might have questioned the origin and meaning of life. Commissioned by EMI Classic's president, Richard Lyttelton, to celebrate the company's centenary, it was released on CD, plus a limited 2-disc vinyl edition, and made it to the top of the classical charts. Premiered at the Royal Albert Hall, a BBC documentary *The Making of Standing Stone* is available on DVD.

Working Classical

Released:	1 November 1999
Label:	EMI Classics
Producer:	John Fraser
Recorded:	Abbey Road Studios
UK:	No. 99
USA:	Did not chart

Working Classical (pointing a light-hearted finger at Paul's Liverpool upbringing) primarily took some of his existing numbers (including 'My Love' and 'Maybe I'm Amazed') and converted them into orchestral adaptations (something which had been done many times in the past, although in a lighter tone, by the likes of James Last and Bert Kaempfert, filling £1 record bins in charity shops across the UK in later years). McCartney also wrote some new pieces ('Haymakers', 'Midwife', 'Spiral' and 'Tuesday') with all arrangements new and old performed by the London Symphony Orchestra and the Loma Mar Quartet, recorded once again at Abbey Road. Another No. 1 in the classical charts, although barely making a dent in the official UK/US album charts.

Ecce Cor Meum

Released:	25 September 2006
Label:	EMI Classics
Producer:	John Fraser
Recorded:	Abbey Road Studios
UK:	Did not chart
USA:	Did not chart

Behold My Heart (English translation of the Latin title) was written by Paul (partially in devotion to his wife Linda), an oratorio in four movements, scored for and performed by soprano Kate Royal, the boys of Magdalen College Choir, Oxford, the boys of King's College, Cambridge Choir, London Voices and the Academy of St Martin-in-the-Fields Orchestra, conducted by Gavin Greenaway. Paul had been asked to write a new piece for Magdalen College by its president Anthony Smith in celebration of a new concert hall for the college. Sadly the composition was delayed by the death of Linda in 1998, but was finished and eventually performed in the Sheldonian Theatre, Oxford, in November 2001. The premières took place in November 2006 at a sold-out Royal Albert Hall in London and Carnegie Hall in New York. It won Best Album Award from *Classic FM* magazine and reached No. 2 in the UK classical charts.

Ocean's Kingdom (Choreography By Peter Martins)

Released:	3 October 2011
Label:	Decca/Hear Music
Producer:	John Fraser
Recorded:	Henry Wood Hall, London
UK:	Did not chart
USA:	Did not chart

McCartney's fifth classical album and first ballet piece, *Ocean's Kingdom* was commissioned by the New York City Ballet, performed by the London Classical Orchestra and conducted by John Wilson. The ballet is based on a love story in four orchestral movements that take place in two mystical worlds – the good Ocean Kingdom and bad Earth Kingdom – which results in the underwater way of life being threatened. Released on CD and vinyl, the album can also be downloaded from iTunes containing the studio version and a live performance from the world première in September 2011 at the Fall Gala by the New York City Ballet Orchestra, conducted by Fayçal Karoui. Topped the US classical chart and No. 4 in the UK equivalent.

Ambient, Electronic, Mash-Up & Remix Albums

Strawberries Oceans Ships Forest (The Fireman)

Released:	15 November 1993
Label:	Parlophone/Capitol
Producer:	The Fireman
Recorded:	Hog Hill Mill Studios, Icklesham, East Sussex
UK:	Did not chart
USA:	Did not chart

The first of McCartney's ambient/electronic mash-up albums put together by himself and Martin Glover, better known as Youth. The project got underway when Paul asked Youth to remix several tracks from the *Off the Ground* album, plus two tracks – 'Reception' and 'The Broadcast' – from Wings' 1979 album *Back to the Egg*. Originally planned as a series of 12-inch singles, McCartney loved the results so much that he decided to release them as an anonymous album. Although it did not chart, the album was very well received by the media: "staggeringly brilliant", as *Melody Maker* described it.

Rushes (The Fireman)

Released:	21 September 1998
Label:	Hydra/EMI
Producer:	The Fireman
Recorded:	Hog Hill Mill Studios, Icklesham, East Sussex
UK:	Did not chart
USA:	Did not chart

The second of Paul and Martin Glover's Fireman albums, this time with all new and unused material from McCartney's archive. Movingly, although coping with the last few weeks of her life, Linda McCartney remained involved and encouraging all the way through the project. In an interview Martin Glover said proudly, "When I listen to the album now, it sounds like a requiem for her, it's very beautiful."

Liverpool Sound Collage

Released:	21 August 2000
Label:	Hydra/Capitol
Producer:	Paul McCartney
Recorded:	Hog Hill Mill Studios, Icklesham, East Sussex
UK:	Did not chart
USA:	Did not chart

When the artist Peter Blake (responsible for the cover of the Beatles' *Sgt. Pepper's Lonely Hearts Club Band* LP) put together an artwork exhibition in Liverpool, he asked McCartney to come up with some music in keeping with his art and the city. Paul's answer was to combine old Beatles chitchat during recording sessions with snippets of his 1991 classical *Liverpool Oratorio* to create the album. He can also be heard walking through Liverpool's streets asking local people to explain what Liverpool and the Beatles mean to them. (Although primarily Paul McCartney's work, the album is also credited to the Beatles, Super Furry Animals and Youth.) The album was nominated for the 2001 Grammy Award for 'Best Alternative Music Album'.

Twin Freaks (With The Freelance Hellraiser)

Released:	13 June 2005
Label:	Parlophone
Producer:	Freelance Hellraiser
Recorded:	Hog Hill Mill Studios, Icklesham, East Sussex
UK:	Did not chart
USA:	Did not chart

A double vinyl album put together by Paul McCartney and Roy Kerr, better known as Freelance Hellraiser – an English DJ, musician, producer, remixer and one of the creators of the UK mash-up music scene. Kerr had collaborated with Paul during his 2004 '04 Summer Tour' when Freelance Hellraiser performed a 30-minute set of dramatically remixed McCartney tracks prior to the shows. So impressed was McCartney, *Twin Freaks* was the outcome. The album cover features one of Paul's paintings.

Electric Arguments (The Fireman)

Released:	24 November 2008
Label:	One Little Indian/ATO
Producer:	The Fireman
Recorded:	Hog Hill Mill Studios, Icklesham, East Sussex
UK:	No. 79
USA:	No. 67

The third of the Fireman albums recorded by McCartney and Youth, it's the first to include prominent vocals (from McCartney), the first to display the performers' names on the cover and the first to make it into the UK and US charts. Recorded in just 13 days (spread over a year), McCartney said in an interview with *Rolling Stone* magazine that he sang all of the songs "with absolutely no concept of what the melody or lyrics would be about. So it was like writing on the spot, which I think lent an electricity to the whole sound." In its review of the album *Rolling Stone* agreed, describing it as "the ex-Beatle's headiest music in years".

Right: *Promotional event at London's HMV record store for the Fireman's 'Electric Arguments', December 2008*

Paul McCartney/Wings 50 Highest Ranking Singles Over The Last Six Decades

Hundreds of Wings and Paul McCartney singles exist around the world – far too many to include here. Instead, here are his 50 top-ranking singles, in reverse order, using calculations based on sales figures (physical, digital and streaming), chart positions and international popularity polls.

Only records written (or co-written) by Paul McCartney and performed by him as the major artist are included. Guest performances by McCartney are not included.

All songs written by Paul McCartney unless stated otherwise.

50. This One/The First Stone (McCartney/Stuart)

Parlophone/Capitol 1989
From: *Flowers in the Dirt*
UK: 18   **US: 94**

A mid-tempo love song asking everyone to respect karma and seize the moment, this moment, rather than wait for a better one that may never come. The B-side (the first song co-written with Hamish Stuart) covers a similar religious theme of sinners casting the first stone.

49. Arrow Through Me/Old Siam, Sir

Columbia 1979
From: *Back to the Egg*
UK: Not released   **US: 29**

A nice soul-funk piece and one of the best tracks from Wings' rather disappointing final album. The B-side 'Old Siam, Sir' had already been released as a UK single and made it to No. 35 in the charts. Drummer Steve Holley actually came up with the chord sequence but was not credited.

48. Put it There/Mama's Little Girl

Parlophone 1990
From: *Flowers in the Dirt*
UK: 32   **US: Did not chart**

Acoustic folk song based on father/son relationships, with the title from a phrase his father would use when shaking hands: "Put it there if it weighs a ton." The B-side is another nice folky song from the 1972 *Red Rose Speedway* sessions and appears on the original double album.

47. The Back Seat of My Car/Heart of the Country (Paul/Linda McCartney)

Apple 1971
From: *Ram*
UK: 39   **US: Not released**

The UK release of the final track from *Ram* – one of McCartney's classic road numbers with its sexual connotations of young couples

Discography

escaping to spend time alone. 'Heart of the Country', co-written with Linda, reflected their search for a simpler life in Scotland.

46. Dance Tonight/Nod Your Head

Hear Music/MPL 2007

From: *Memory Almost Full*

UK: 26   **US: 69**

A folky mandolin number released on 18 June 2007 (Paul's 65th birthday), originally only as a download. It wasn't actually released in the USA but still made it to No. 69 in the Hot 100. Nice one to skip around to.

45. Jenny Wren/Summer of '59

Parlophone 2005

From: *Chaos and Creation in the Backyard*

UK: 22   **US: Not released**

One of McCartney's best acoustic ballads for some time but was not released in the USA and surprisingly only made it to No. 22 in the UK. Includes a lovely solo on a duduk (Armenian woodwind instrument) played by Venezuelan musician Pedro Eustache.

44. Figure of Eight/Ou Est le Soleil?

Parlophone 1989

From: *Flowers in the Dirt*

UK: 42   **US: 92**

Sounding remarkably like the late '90s US indie band the New Radicals (this arrived nine years earlier and must have been an influence), it's a great track with McCartney's vocals at their best. Funky B-side was a bonus track on the album's CD release the following year.

43. Beautiful Night/Love Come Tumbling Down

Parlophone 1997

From: *Flaming Pie*

UK: 25   **US: Not released**

The Beatles Anthology hadn't even had the time to cool down before this arrived: Paul, Ringo on drums and backing vocals, George Martin handling the orchestration and Jeff Lynne at the controls. Mid-tempo

ballad is transformed into a Beatles rocker.

42. Tropic Island Hum/We All Stand Togother

Parlophone/MPL 2004

From: *Tropical Island Hum* (animation)

UK: 21   **US: Not released**

Surprising that this children's song sold reasonably well, given a lot of people hadn't heard it (well, I hadn't - my kids had grown up by then). No idea what it's all about, but something to do with Wirral the Squirrel bonging on a bongo.

41. Fine Line/Growing Up Falling Down

Parlophone 2005

From: *Chaos and Creation in the Backyard*

UK: 20   **US: Did not chart**

Opening track from *Chaos and Creation in the Backyard*, the title comes from an idea in Paul's mind that there's a fine line between courage and recklessness. Written during the same sessions, the North African-influenced B-side again features multi-instrumentalist Pedro Eustache.

40. Young Boy/Looking For You

Parlophone 1997

From: *Flaming Pie*

UK: 19   **US: Not released**

'Young Boy' was written by Paul, he says, "in the time that it took Linda to cook a lunch". Drawing comparisons between his own early life and a young boy today starting out on the journey, he recorded it six months later at Steve Miller's home studio in Sun Valley, Idaho. 'Looking For You' was the result of a loose studio jam with Ringo and Jeff Lynne during the *Flaming Pie* sessions.

39. Venus and Mars + Rock Show/Magneto and Titanium Man

Capitol 1975

From: *Venus and Mars*

UK: Not released   **US: 12**

A great opener from the album to convey the excitement and

anticipation of a rock gig and good enough to become Wings' show opener for several years. B-side is based on Marvel Comics characters (McCartney is a fan), which was also performed live with the characters projected onto a stage screen.

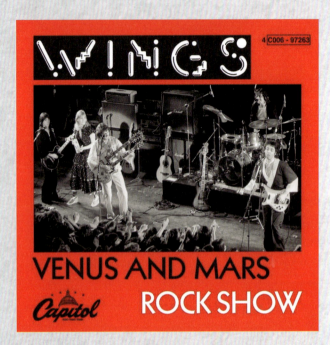

38. Once Upon a Long Ago/Back on My Feet (McCartney/MacManus)
Parlophone/MPL 1987
From: *All the Best!*
UK: 10   **US: Not released**

Looking back to a time when life was simpler, this slow ballad was intended to be recorded with Queen's Freddie Mercury, but sadly never happened. Instead it was added as an original number to Paul's *All the Best!* compilation. Features a nice violin solo from Nigel Kennedy. B-side is the first release from songwriting sessions with Elvis Costello – piano-based, musical-style number.

37. The World Tonight/Used to be Bad
Parlophone/Capitol 1997
From: *Flaming Pie*
UK: 23   **US: 64**

Jeff Lynne's influence is clear from the first note of this number from *Flaming Pie*, with the two of them taking care of all instruments.

Theme is another good example of Paul looking back on his life. B-side is the excellent blues-rock number co-written with Steve Miller, who shares the vocals.

36. London Town (McCartney/Laine)/I'm Carrying
Parlophone/Capitol 1978
From: *London Town*
UK: 60   **US: 39**

Written initially while in Australia during a Wings world tour, and completed with Denny Laine on a sunny day in Scotland, the song reflects ordinary people going about their lives in a typically overcast and drizzly London. B-side is a love ballad actually written about a former girlfriend.

35. Waterfalls/Check My Machine
Parlophone/Columbia 1980
From: *McCartney II*
UK: 9   **US: Did not chart**

Considered by Paul's ballad-fans, not surprisingly, as the best song on *McCartney II*, but strangely did not chart in the USA's Billboard Hot 100. 'Check My Machine' is a funky number also from the *McCartney II* sessions and preferable to some that did make it onto the album.

34. Press/It's Not True
Parlophone 1986
From: *Press to Play*
UK: 25   **US: 21**

A below average song from a well-below average album, ruined by its overpowering gated-reverb drum effect and a variety of other annoying sound effects that contribute nothing. The slower, soulful ballad 'It's Not True' is preferable, until those damned drums make a comeback.

33. Letting Go/You Gave Me the Answer
Capitol 1975
From: *Venus and Mars*
UK: 41   **US: 39**

A soulful blues-rock number that draws comparisons with the

Beatles' 'Oh! Darling' from *Abbey Road*. On the B-side is another of Paul's witty and enjoyable crooner ditties in tribute to his father, James, written and recorded in the style of Cole Porter.

32. Mary Had a Little Lamb/Little Woman Love (Both Paul/Linda McCartney)

Apple 1972

Single only

UK: 9   US: 28

Another song written for children – his own, in fact, who happily join in on the vocals – based on the words of a well-known nursery rhyme of the same name. Not surprisingly slated by the critics but sold reasonably well. The rockabilly B-side from the *Ram* sessions is just about preferable.

31. Getting Closer/Baby's Request

Parlophone/Columbia 1979

From: *Back to the Egg*

UK: 60   US: 20

Another double A-side single, and the last from Wings, the record deserved better sales. 'Getting Closer' is a good up-tempo number similar in many ways to UK bands such as Squeeze; 'Baby's Request' was actually written for the US harmony quartet, the Mills Brothers, but ended up on *Back to the Egg* – a nice, Thirties-style, jazzy croon number.

30. I've Had Enough/Deliver Your Children (McCartney/Laine)

Parlophone/Capitol 1978

From: *London Town*

UK: 42   US: 25

A straight raucous rocker from the generally folkier *London Town* album, but one of the best songs lifted from it, poking a critical finger at problems in relationships. Denny Laine handles lead vocals on the pleasantly folky B-side – a great song sounding remarkably like the Levellers!

29. Give Ireland Back to the Irish (Paul & Linda McCartney)/(Instrumental version)

Apple 1972

Single only

UK: 16   US: 21

Wings' first single released in February 1972 in response to the dreadful events on 'Bloody Sunday' in Northern Ireland just a few days earlier. Banned by the BBC and largely ignored by US radio, nevertheless the song sold well and, unsurprisingly, made it to No. 1 in Ireland.

28. My Brave Face/Flying To My Home (Both McCartney/MacManus)

Parlophone/Capitol 1989

From: *Flowers in the Dirt*

UK: 18   US: 25

The first single from *Flowers in the Dirt* and a good choice as one of the better songs from the album, co-written with Elvis Costello, concerning a man struggling to take care of himself after a relationship comes to an end. Unusual B-side, which doesn't really sound like Paul at all, but a decent song.

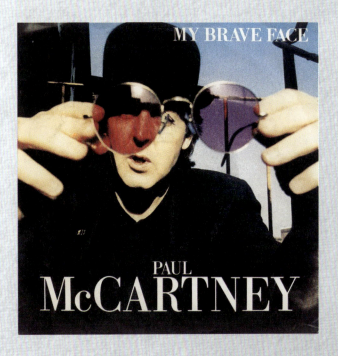

27. Wonderful Christmastime/Rudolph the Red-Nosed Reggae (Johnny Marks)

Parlophone/Columbia 1979

Single only

UK: 6 **US: 28**

One of those Christmas hits – up there with the likes of Slade's 'Merry Xmas Everybody' – that reappears every year from about October onwards, and remains very popular. Recorded by Paul alone during the *McCartney II* sessions. The B-side is a comical reggae instrumental version of Johnny Mark's classic 'Rudolph the Red-Nosed Reindeer'.

26. Tug of War/Get It

Parlophone/Columbia 1982

From: *Tug of War*

UK: 53 **US: 53**

Title number from Paul's first (proper) solo album since Wings had split, it's an overly emotional protest song drawing attention to world conflicts and the hope that things will improve, with lush orchestration handled by George Martin. The B-side is a more cheerful rockabilly duet with one of Paul's heroes, guitarist Carl Perkins.

25. Hope of Deliverance/Long Leather Coat (Paul/Linda McCartney)

Parlophone/Capitol 1992

From: *Off the Ground*

UK: 18 **US: 83**

Written by Paul up in his loft for a bit of peace and quiet one day, the song with its Latin vibe represents hopeful optimism in a troubled world, but for some reason was received much more successfully in the UK than the USA. Rockier B-side 'Long Leather Coat' is an animal rights protest number written with Linda.

24. Spies Like Us/My Carnival (Paul/Linda McCartney)

Parlophone/Capitol 1985

From: *Spies Like Us* (film)

UK: 13 **US: 7**

Funky title song for the Chevy Chase and Dan Aykroyd spoof spy movie. Quite a funny film. Quite a good theme tune. But nothing more. For some reason Paul's theme tune wasn't included on the movie soundtrack, composed and directed by Elmer Bernstein. B-side was written during the New Orleans Mardi Gras Carnival, which they had attended disguised as clowns.

23. We All Stand Together/(Humming Version)

Parlophone 1984

From: *Rupert and the Frog Song* (animation)

UK: 3 **US: Not released**

A song about the much-loved UK children's comic strip character Rupert the Bear, created by Kent artist Mary Tourtel in 1920 for the *Daily Express* newspaper, where it still appears to this day. Like most UK children, Paul was a big fan, and still is, and had intended to write this song since 1978 for an animated film for children – and what's wrong with that, either? Many critics, as usual, disagreed.

22. Take it Away/I'll Give You a Ring

Parlophone/Columbia 1982

From: *Tug of War*

UK: 15 **US: 10**

A mid-tempo number initially intended for Wings, this final version features two drummers – Ringo and top session player Steve Gadd – and George Martin on piano helping to create a terrific, happy, soulful pop song. B-side is one of Paul's lesser-known songs written in the early '70s – a lovely, whimsical, music hall-style singalong with some great clarinet solos by Tony Coe.

21. Pipes Of Peace/So Bad

Parlophone 1983

From: *Pipes of Peace*

UK: 1   **US: Not released**

Further differences between UK and USA record companies as to which was the best A-side led to overall sales being affected. 'Pipes of Peace', based on the well-known Christmas Day truce between British and German soldiers during WWI, made it to No. 1 in the UK. 'So Sad', a family love song and not a particularly good one, only reached No. 23 as the US A-side preference.

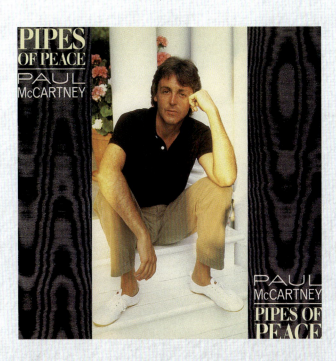

20. Helen Wheels/Country Dreamer (Both Paul/Linda McCartney)

Apple 1973

Single only

UK: 12   **US: 10**

A Chuck Berry-style road song that was actually written about Paul and Linda's Land Rover up in Scotland and the regular journey they made back down to London. Not quite as cool as 'Maybellene' on Route 66, but not bad. The nice country and western 'Country Dreamer' love song was planned for inclusion on the double album version of *Red Rose Speedway*.

19. Junior's Farm/Sally G (Both Paul/Linda McCartney)

Apple 1974

Single only

UK: 16   **US: 3**

Influenced by Bob Dylan's 'Maggie's Farm', this was Wings' attempt at country rock to tick yet another box, and a pretty good job they do of it, too, recorded during time spent in Nashville. The country music-influenced B-side 'Sally G' also made it separately into the USA Hot 100, peaking at No. 17.

18. Hi Hi Hi/C Moon (Both Paul/Linda McCartney)

Apple 1972

Double A-side single

UK: 5   **US: 10**

A good rock 'n' roll number that's always remembered for being banned by the BBC because of the word 'Hi', seen to encourage the use of drugs; the lyrics, however, are so sexually graphic that it's a wonder 'Hi' was ever noticed. Reggae-influenced C Moon slots in perfectly as the B-side; all about a young person trying to be cool, it includes a reference to filling 'my head with glue'. The BBC might have missed that one...

17. Maybe I'm Amazed (Live)/Soily (Live) (Paul/Linda McCartney)

Capitol 1977

From: *Wings Over America*

UK: 28   **US: 10**

Two live numbers taken from the *Wings Over America* triple album. Strange this standout track from *McCartney* wasn't released as a single back in 1970, but Paul stuck to his morals in believing that was ripping off the fans. The live version was recorded at a show in Kansas City while the rocky B-side, 'Soily', was used as the show-closer from a performance in Denver.

16. Goodnight Tonight/Daytime Nighttime Suffering

Parlophone/Columbia 1979

Single only

UK: 5   US: 5

Originally recorded for *Back to the Egg* but eventually released as a flamenco-influenced disco-dance single. The song achieved Top 5 status in both the UK/USA charts, with an accompanying video showing the band having fun dressed in Thirties outfits. The B-side slot was up for grabs for anyone who could come up with a suitable number; in the end, of course, it was McCartney.

15. Jet/Let Me Roll It (Both Paul/Linda McCartney)

Apple 1974

From: *Band on the Run*

UK: 7   US: 7

Is it about Paul's black puppy, or his black pony? Explanations vary, but does it matter? The lyrics make very little sense anyway, so why should the title? But in T. Rex-style, it all comes together and works pretty well. Great B-side as well; should've sold more.

14. No More Lonely Nights (Ballad)/ (Playout Version)

Parlophone/Columbia 1984

From: *Give My Regards to Broad Street*

UK: 2   US: 6

One of the few decent things to be found on Paul's silly brain-fade comedy movie. Not a bad song, and sold well on both sides of the Atlantic, but two versions of it on a single are more than enough. Recorded at Elstree Film Studios in north London as one of only three original songs for the movie.

13. Uncle Albert/Admiral Halsey (Paul/Linda McCartney)/Too Many People

Apple 1971

From: *Ram*

UK: Not released   US: 1

One of the highlights on the wonderful *Ram*, but only released in the USA for some reason, this is one of McCartney's best examples of mashing together various short song fragments to create something brilliant. (Norwegian engineer Eirik Wangberg should take some of the credit.) Sold 1.5 million copies, while the B-side has a dig at John and Yoko.

12. Mull of Kintyre (McCartney/Laine)/ Girls' School

Capitol 1977

Double A-side single

UK: 1   US: 33

Paul and Denny Laine sat outside on a sunny day in the Scottish hills with their guitars and a bottle of whisky and produced one of the biggest-selling singles of all time, selling more than 4 million copies. In the UK, anyway. The Scots (or Americans) in the USA didn't buy too many, probably because radio presenters preferred to play the alternative A-side. Puzzling, because this would probably have been our No. 1; double A-side singles often backfire.

11. Another Day (Paul/Linda McCartney) /Oh Woman Oh Why

Apple 1971

Single only

UK: 2   US: 5

McCartney's first solo single was chosen from the *Ram* sessions, rather than taking its deserved place on the album, but a great choice – a folky description of a lonely girl's daily dull routine. Brilliant. The B-side would have fitted on *Ram* just as comfortably, and these two numbers plus a few more additions such as 'I Lie Around' could have resulted in a wonderful double album.

instantly bangs out one of the best Bond themes ever. Reggae middle-8 section was actually Linda's idea. B-side 'I Lie Around', recorded in 1970, deserves better and should've made it onto a *Ram* double.

10. Let 'Em In/Beware My Love (Both Paul/Linda McCartney)

Capitol 1976

From: *Wings At the Speed of Sound*

UK: 2 **US: 3**

A cool opening number from Wings' excellent *Wings at the Speed of Sound*, it's basically an invitation to a party round at Paul's place – including family members (Brother Michael and Auntie Gin) and famous friends such as the Everly Brothers and even Martin Luther. And a great rocking B-side.

9. Live and Let Die/I Lie Around (Both Paul/Linda McCartney)

Apple 1973

From: *Live and Let Die* (film and soundtrack)

UK: 9 **US: 2**

We've been waiting for you, Mr. McCartney! Nothing like the sort of material we'd expect from him, but Paul reads Ian Fleming's novel and

8. With a Little Luck/Backwards Traveller + Cuff Link

Parlophone/Capitol 1978

From: *London Town*

UK: 5 **US: 1**

The follow-up song to the UK's best ever selling single (at the time) 'Mull of Kintyre', this one had some big shoes to fill but was sufficiently successful to make it to No. 1 in the USA, where it stayed for two weeks. 'Backwards Traveller/Cuff Link' on the B-side is a medley of two short songs also from *London Town*. The instrumental 'Cuff Link', once again, sounds very similar to the 'Zoo Gang' theme tune (see No. 4).

7. Listen to What the Man Said/Love in Song (Both Paul/Linda McCartney)

Capitol 1975

From: *Venus and Mars*

UK: 6 **US: 1**

Another No. 1 in the USA, if only for a week, 'Listen to What the Man

Said' is a great number capturing the vibe of New Orleans, where it was recorded during the *Venus and Mars* sessions. Paul brought in Traffic's Dave Mason to add guitar overdubs while Tom Scott came up with a fantastic saxophone solo. B-side 'Love in Song', a lovely acoustic ballad, is equally impressive.

6. Coming Up/(Live Version) + Lunchbox/ Odd Sox (Paul/Linda McCartney)

Parlophone/Columbia 1980

From: *McCartney II*

UK: 2   **US: 1**

An unexpected success given its lo-fi production values and quirky vibe, but the best thing on *McCartney II*. Fans loved it, especially Wings' rockier version on the B-side, recorded live at the Glasgow Apollo; once again, the B-side enjoyed considerably more radio plays in the USA than the studio version and spent three weeks at No. 1. The bonus 'Lunchbox/Odd Sox' is a decent knees-up instrumental. Very similar to 'Zoo Gang' – in fact, probably a better theme tune.

5. My Love/The Mess (Both Paul/Linda McCartney)

Apple 1973

From: *Red Rose Speedway*

UK: 9   **US: 1**

One of McCartney's best ever love songs (and there are plenty of them to choose from). Even without Henry McCullough's brilliant guitar solo it's a great song. With it... sublime - up there with George Harrison's 'Something'. 'The Mess' was recorded live at The Hague in the Netherlands and would have appeared on *Red Rose Speedway* if it had remained a double album.

4. Band on the Run/Zoo Gang (Both Paul/Linda McCartney)

Apple 1974

From: *Band on the Run*

UK: 3   **US: 1**

The three-section opening number on Wings' best album, recorded in a shack in Lagos by three deserted, depressed musicians, still made it to No. 1 (for a week) in the USA. A miracle. Could have made two great songs – possibly even three. The B-side is the theme to a British TV drama, *Zoo Gang,* starring John Mills; neither the theme tune nor the series were particularly good.

3. Ebony and Ivory/Rainclouds (McCartney/Laine)

Parlophone/Columbia 1982

From: *Tug of War*

UK: 1   **US: 1**

McCartney's first collaborated duet performance on a single, this with Stevie Wonder as a black and white love-in protest against racism. A bit sloppy, maybe, but powerful enough to get banned in South Africa, and to spend seven weeks at No. 1 on the Billboard Hot 100 and three weeks in the UK. Despite being Paul's only double No. 1 solo single, it has sold fewer copies overall than our chart's top two hits.

2. Silly Love Songs/Cook of the House (Both Paul/Linda McCartney)

Capitol 1976

From: *Wings at the Speed of Sound*

UK: 2   **US: 1**

McCartney's response to anyone who dared to criticise his work as being too lightweight. And a disco number, at that! Spent five weeks at No. 1 in the US Hot 100 and sold over 3 million copies. As Paul would say: "What's wrong with that?" B-side 'Cook of the House' was co-written by Paul and Linda, with Linda taking lead vocals for the first time with Wings

1. Say Say Say (McCartney/Jackson)/ Ode to a Koala Bear

Parlophone/Columbia 1983

From: *Pipes of Peace*

UK: 2   US: 1

Co-written and performed with Michael Jackson, and lead single from *Pipes of Peace*, this was their second collaboration together after 'The Girl is Mine' a year or so earlier. Has sold over 4.5 million copies worldwide and spent six weeks at No. 1 in America. On a very sad note, 'Ode to a Koala Bear' was the last song Paul recorded while John Lennon was still alive. He was murdered later that day in New York on 8 December 1980.

Above: Michael Jackson, Kim Wilde, Pete Townshend and Paul McCartney at the BRIT awards, London, 16th February 1983

Acknowledgements & Sources

Once again there's an awful lot of Beatles and Paul McCartney published material out there, but the following books, periodicals, films and websites have provided invaluable in-depth information and quotations. All are highly recommended:

Books

Badman, Keith — *The Beatles After the Break-Up 1970-2000: A day-by-day diary*

Beatles, The — *The Beatles Anthology*

Beatles, The — *Get Back*

Benson, Ross — *Paul McCartney: Behind the Myth*

Blaney, John — *Lennon and McCartney Together Alone: A critical discography of their solo work*

Chrisp, Pete — *The Beatles on Vinyl*

DiLello, Richard — *The Longest Cocktail Party*

Doyle, Tom — *Man on the Run: Paul McCartney in the 1970s*

Du Noyer, Paul — *Conversations with McCartney*

Emerick, Geoff &
Massey, Howard — *Here, There and Everywhere: My Life Recording the Music of the Beatles*

Fearon, Gary — *After Abbey Road: The Solo Hits of the Beatles*

Hepworth, David — *Abbey Road NW8: The Inside Story of the World's Most Famous Recording Studio*

Higgs, John — *Love and Let Die: Bond, the Beatles and the British Psyche*

Johns, Glyn — *Sound Man*

Kozinn, Allan &
Sinclair, Adrian — *The McCartney Legacy: Volume 1: 1969-73*

Lewisohn, Mark — *The Complete Beatles Chronicle*

McCabe, Peter &
Schonfeld, Robert D. — *Apple to the Core: The Unmaking of the Beatles*

McCartney, Paul — *The Lyrics*

McNab, Ken — *And in the End: The Last Days of the Beatles*

Miles, Barry — *Paul McCartney: Many Years From Now*

Norman, Philip — *Paul McCartney: The Biography*

Perasi, Luca — *Paul McCartney: Recording Sessions (1969-2013): A Journey Through Paul McCartney's Songs After the Beatles*

Sounes, Howard — *FAB: An Intimate Life of Paul McCartney*

Visconti, Tony — *The Autobiography: Bowie, Bolan and the Brooklyn Boy*

Wilson, Terry — *Four Sides of the Circle: The Beatles' Second Phase, 1970-1974*

Womack, Kenneth — *Sound Pictures: The Life of Beatles Producer George Martin. The Later Years 1966-2016*

Newspapers

(London publications unless location indicated)

Daily Mail

Daily Mirror

Daily Telegraph

Evening Standard

Guardian

Independent

New York Times

Sunday Times

Times

Periodicals

Billboard

Classic Pop

Classic Rock

Club Sandwich

Melody Maker

Mojo

New Musical Express

Q

Record Mirror

Record Collector

Rolling Stone

Uncut

Television/video/DVD

A&E Television Networks/MPL Communications 2005 – *Paul McCartney in Red Square*

A&E Television Networks/MPL Communications 2006 – *Paul McCartney: The Space Within US: A Concert Film*

Apple Corps/EMI Records/ITV 1995 – *The Beatles Anthology*

BBC Arena/Grounded Productions/Eagle Rock Entertainment 2011 – *Produced by George Martin*

Acknowledgements And Sources

British Lion Films 1966/StudioCanal 2020 – *The Family Way* (Featuring music by Paul McCartney)

Coach House Productions 2021 – *McCartney: Now and Then*

Disney/Apple Corps/WingNut Films 2021 – *The Beatles: Get Back* (Peter Jackson's 8hr documentary of the making of the 1970 *Let it Be* album and film)

Disney/Ventureland/Mercury Studios 2022 – *If These Walls Could Sing* (Documentary on Abbey Road Studios directed by Mary McCartney)

Eagle Rock Entertainment 2011 – *Paul McCartney: The Love We Make*

Eagle Rock Entertainment 2018 – *Paul McCartney and Wings: Rockshow*

Hulu 2021 – *McCartney 3,2,1*

Liberty 2006 – *Paul McCartney: Paul is Live in Concert on the New World Tour*

Miramax 2004 – *Paul McCartney: The Music and Animation Collection*

MPL Communications 1984 – *Give My Regards to Broad Street*

MPL Communications 1997 – *In the World Tonight*

MPL Communications 2001 – *Wingspan: An Intimate Portrait*

MPL Communications/Capitol Records 2002 – *Paul McCartney: Back in the U.S. Concert Film*

MPL Communications/Hear Music/Universal Music/Concord Music Group 2009 – *Good Evening New York City: Paul McCartney's Historic Citi Field Opening Show*

MPL Communications/Hear Music/Universal Music/Concord Music Group 2012 – *Rammed: The Album Story*

MPL Communications/Capitol Records/Done + Dusted Productions/BBC 2020 – *Paul McCartney: Live at the Cavern Club*

Prism Films 2011 – *Strange Fruit: The Beatles' Apple Records*

Showbox Home Entertainment 2006 – *Put it There*

Voodoo Video 2022 – *Paul McCartney: Glastonbury*

Warner Music Entertainment/MPL Communications 2007 – *The McCartney Years*

Web sites

abbeyroad.com
albumlinernotes.com
allmusic.com
beatlesbible.com
beatlesbooks.com
beatlesdiscs.blogspot.com
beatleswiki.com
billboard.com

discogs.com
magnetmagazine.com
marklewisohn.net
mojo4music.com
nme.com
paulmccartney.com
qthemusic.com
recordcollectormag.com

rockcellarmagazine.com
rollingstone.com
sussexlive.co.uk
teamrock.com
the-paulmccartney-project.com
ultimateclassicrock.com
uncut.co.uk
webgrafikk.com (The Daily Beatle)

Pete Chrisp has worked as a writer and editor for newspapers, magazines and books since 1979. His books include the highly acclaimed *Riding Shotgun*, co-written with Rory Gallagher's bass player, Gerry McAvoy; best-selling *The Beatles on Vinyl*; and the recently revised and updated *Don't Stop: 55 Years of Fleetwood Mac*. He has also edited myriad music books across a wide range of topics – from the Byrds and folk music through to tube amps and collectable guitars. He lives in Kent, England.

For their help, advice and encouragement, many thanks to Gary O'Neill, Juliette O'Neill, Huw Thomas, Carolyn McHugh and Sally Beeby.

What's it all about... Alfie? Nina? Archie? Flo? ...?